WISDOM OF THE AGES

REVELATIONS FROM ZERTOULEM THE PROPHET OF TLASKANATA

By Rev. George A. Fuller, M. D.

First published in 1916

Published by Left of Brain Books

Copyright © 2023 Left of Brain Books

ISBN 978-1-396-32310-2

First Edition

All rights reserved. No part of this publication may be reproduced, distributed, or transmitted in any form or by any means, including photocopying, recording, or other electronic or mechanical methods, without the prior written permission of the publisher, except in the case of brief quotations permitted by copyright law. Left of Brain Books is a division of Left Of Brain Onboarding Pty Ltd.

PUBLISHER'S PREFACE

About the Book

"This book, a product of automatic writing, first came to my attention in a footnote in William James' Varieties of Religious Experience. James compared this text to Oahspe, as well as the case of Helene Smith, described in From India to the Planet Mars. The book claims to be the revelation of one Zertoulem, who lived long ago in a land called Tlaskanata. The preface and glossary state that Tlaskanata was in Middle America, 'thousands of years ago.'

The actual text is a lot more consistent than most automatic writing I've seen. The style is similar to Lord Dunsany, Khalil Gibran, or perhaps the orientalist translations of Edward Fitz-Gerald. Although the setting is in a previously unknown lost civilization, the spiritual concerns addressed here are very modern. As far as I can tell this book has not been reprinted since 1916.

(Quote from sacred-texts.com)

CONTENTS

PUBLISHER'S PREFACE
INTRODUCTION 1
    CHAPTER I. 4
    CHAPTER II. 6
    CHAPTER III. 8
    CHAPTER IV. 10
    CHAPTER V. 12
    CHAPTER VI. 14
    CHAPTER VII. 16
    CHAPTER VIII. 18
    CHAPTER IX. 20
    CHAPTER X. 23
    CHAPTER XI. 25
    CHAPTER XII. 27
    CHAPTER XIII. 29
    CHAPTER XIV. 31
    CHAPTER XV. 33
    CHAPTER XVI. 35
    CHAPTER XVII. 37
    CHAPTER XVIII. 39
    CHAPTER XIX. 41
    CHAPTER XX. 43
    CHAPTER XXI. 45
    CHAPTER XXII. 48
    CHAPTER XXIII. 50
    CHAPTER XXIV. 52
    CHAPTER XXV. 54
    CHAPTER XXVI. 56
    CHAPTER XXVII. 58
    CHAPTER XXVIII. 60
    CHAPTER XXIX. 62
    CHAPTER XXX. 64
    CHAPTER XXXI. 66
    CHAPTER XXXII. 68
    CHAPTER XXXIII. 71
    CHAPTER XXXIV. 73
    CHAPTER XXXV. 76
    CHAPTER XXXVI. 79
    CHAPTER XXXVII. 82

- CHAPTER XXXVIII. 85
- CHAPTER XXXIX. 88
- CHAPTER XL. 91
- CHAPTER XLI. 94
- CHAPTER XLII. 97
- CHAPTER XLIII. 99
- CHAPTER XLIV. 102
- CHAPTER XLV. 104
- CHAPTER XLVI. 106
- CHAPTER XLVII. 108
- CHAPTER XLVIII. 110
- CHAPTER XLIX. 112
- CHAPTER L. 114

TLASKAN WORDS 116

INTRODUCTION

TRUTH is eternal, exhaustless, unfathomable. Its Divine Fount is far beyond human discovery, however rich the intellect which aspires towards its inaccessible heights. It lies far above the topmost clouds which eye of man can scan, far beyond the Storm-King's throne, whence the flashing lightnings are hurled, where the mighty thunderbolts are forged; far above the vast waves of ether, that wide Planetary Sea where suns and worlds float and sail their swift, majestic currents; still farther on beyond the boundaries of this entire Universe of expressed Life, toward the Infinite, causeless Cause, the Unmanifest, the Silence, from whose profound depths all vibrations are stirred, all Light spoken, all Harmony breathed—even there and only thence has Truth its pristine, immaculate birth.

No human ear can catch its full-toned syllables, no heart conceive the beauty, the grandeur of its sublime accents, but to the aspiring soul come glintings of its full-orbed Glory, flash-lights of its Perfection. And to that soul which likewise feels its own union with the same wondrous Source, there come in-breathings, or inspirations, of this Eternal Wisdom, whose translation into human speech serves to illumine mundane shadows.

All down through the ages such souls have blessed and enlightened the world. The messages received by such seers, prophets and psalmists have been collected in every cycle of human advancement, into Scriptures fitly termed sacred, into Vedas, Sutras, Koran, Avesta and Bible. No age, nation or teacher holds a copyright above any other for the excellence or infallibility of its particular message. The One Fountain has countless rills, and were all these minute streams collected into one great volume, the vast reservoir which feeds them would still be scarcely touched.

But as humanity advances, as material, grovelling tendencies are transcended and outgrown, and the Light of the Spirit illumines mortal vision, as the yearning of the soul increases and is felt above the clamor of the senses, as the demand for more of Truth arises from the lips and hearts of men, such earnest prayer is always answered. Pure-hearted messengers are chosen and prepared through discipline, through sorrows manifold, to hear this transcendent Voice and transmit its potent accents to mankind.

The planet is now passing its sixth cyclical birthday. The fifth grand cycle wanes, a new spiritual dispensation is upon us; the sixth age advances, the opening of the sixth seal. Our solar centre in his tireless revolution around far distant Alcyone, with his attendant retinue of worlds, passes from one sign of the Zodiac to another, making marked planetary changes in physical, mental and spiritual life. Wars, famine and pestilence abound— the fermentation of unrest, which will work out the necessary purification for the spiritual era, whose dawn already is dimly discerned. Even now the angels of preparation for this glad new Day are on the earth or in the air, psychic gateways are being prepared among the children of men for the entrance of new messages of Truth, for deeper words of Wisdom, for grander pæans of Harmony than have hitherto blessed the world.

Such a message is contained in the rare volume before us, whose origin and manner of transmission are calculated to inspire the soul with reverence and awe. Not alone is it literally the work of angelic hands, but it serves also as a valuable link with a prehistoric past, the inspirer of these pages having once worn mortal form, once trodden mundane pathways, in the earliest civilization our planet has known, many thousand years ago, in Central America.

The instrument through whom this grand, unique message has been transmitted—Dr. George A. Fuller—is admirably fitted to be thus chosen as a mouthpiece of wise inspirers, being a man of pure, clean nature, a close student, philosopher and aspirant for Truth, loving honor and integrity better than fame or fortune. He has been for years before the public as a teacher of spiritual truth, constantly under observation when criticism was rife, without a stain or breath of calumny. Some twenty-five years ago, Dr. Fuller possessed to some degree the gift of automatic writing, and at that time received communications purporting to come from an ancient dweller of Central America. But these messages were chiefly historical and personal, and after a time ceased; gradually also the automatic gift was withdrawn, presumably forever,

After the lapse of a quarter of a century, however,—

> "The mills of the gods grind slow,

But they grind exceeding fine,"

to Dr. Fuller's great surprise, on the morning of June fourth, suddenly and without warning, a peculiar pricking of the hand and arm, with a strong impulse to take his pen, resulted in the transcription of the first chapter in this volume, followed an hour and two hours later by succeeding chapters. At intervals during the current summer, though busily engaged in other absorbing duties, the volume grew, page by page, until the ancient Teacher and Revelator himself pronounced the *Finis*.

Who shall say that other sacred books have not been similarly penned? The manner of inspiration, it is true, matters little, or whether the angel is seen, as it was by John in Patmos, and other early writers; it is the purport of the message which decides its value, and surely the exalted character of this scripture, its revealments of spiritual truth, its advanced teachings, its lofty conceptions and ideals, the beauty of its musical rhythm, the utterly impersonal feature of its authorship, must stamp this work, whatever its source, as pure inspiration of a high order.

By the expressed wish of the intelligence inditing these pages, the volume is now given to the world. The same Power that had a use for it and thus called it into being will direct that those souls who are ready, whose further growth demands this nutriment, will attract it unto them, while minds less ripened may pass it by until a more convenient season. To sow the seed is all the disciple can do. The Lord of the harvest can alone bring the increase in His own time and way. May it prove an hundred-fold to every thoughtful, earnest reader!

"Rise, oh my soul, to still loftier heights; unfettered be all thy wings!"

Susie C. Clark.

CHAPTER I.

ZERTOULEM spake unto the multitude and said: Inasmuch as ye are led by the desire to gratify selfish propensities are ye excluded from the higher light which is the natural birthright of every soul.

Be ye seekers after the higher truths of the spirit, not content with the vain babblings of men who are puffed up with their own self-conceits.

He that overcomes the flesh, not by crucifixion and mortification, but by sublimation, that leadeth to the complete purification of this house in which spirit dwells, shall become a leader among men, and shall know all things in heaven and earth.

Knowledge is not always gained of books, for oft-times these are misleading and unsatisfactory. Spirit must speak to spirit, and soul must vibrate responsive to the inner harmonies of the universe of God.

He who seeks of the spirit shall find the royal road that leadeth to the great garner house where is stored the rich fruitage of the ages.

Be not deceived of men who occupy the chief seats in the synagogues and universities of the outer world, for these are puffed up with their own self-conceits.

They conceive of theories, then search the universe that they may find facts that seem to prove their verity.

They go no deeper than the outer husk of the external universe. Like children, they play with these cast-off shells. Out of these things are builded the sciences and religions of the world.

The teachings of the great masters have been misunderstood and misapplied. The world has been too engrossed with material things to read aright the lessons given.

Only the things of the spirit are permanent. All outward things are transitory and fleeting. Vain pomp and glory of the world without life, ye flaunt your gaudy rags before eyes whose spiritual vision is sealed. Ye have no dominion over him who is baptized of the spirit.

He rises glorified and exalted into the atmosphere of gods.

He reflects no light of sun or star, but glows and shines with the inexhaustible light of spirit.

He acknowledges no leadership, either of book car man, but follows the star of his own destiny.

To, him is given the broadest liberty, for the wings of his spirit, at last, have been unfettered, and now they cleave the ethers of infinite space.

The glory of the rapidly dying East, the wealth of El Dorados, flicker, fade and are lost in this newer glory and wealth of the spirit, exhaustless and undying.

I that speak unto ye am as deathless as the Unspeakable One. I assist at the birth of worlds and universes. I am my own star of destiny.

What I am ye also may become. Through the gateway of suffering and poverty ye must be led until the spirit asserts itself.

Know then your oneness with the Infinite, and claim the royal birthright that is thine inheritance.

CHAPTER II.

WHEN the faithful ones were gathered together Zertoulem appeared in their midst and said unto them: Let peace and love abide ever in your midst.

For without peace there can be no true spiritual growth. It is the foundation upon which all true life must rest. Discord and war are great shadows that shut out the light of Omn the Infinite.

My gospel is one of peace, although at first it might seem to bring discord into the world. For it shall separate families and break many of the ties that the world calls sacred.

Peace cometh not by conforming to the outward usages of the world, but by seeking the way of the spirit that leadeth to a more perfect life.

Wealth and outward prosperity, the inordinate desire for gain, these bring neither peace nor love to the world. Instead they foster the spirit of unrest and develop in man the selfish propensities.

No man has ownership in material things. Houses, lands, books and other properties are loaned him for his use. Not even does he own the body he occupies. This is loaned him for a season, but when Omn calls the spirit hence, he needs must return the body to the great reservoir from whence at the bidding of His spirit it was called.

War is inevitable when man seizes more of this world's goods than he can utilize.

Peace comes when he takes that which he can use for his or other's good.

The earth is Omn's, and the fruits thereof are for the sustenance of his children.

There should be no private ownership in land, but a portion should be set apart by wise leaders sacred to the uses of each individual.

Remember, oh, my disciples, that ye are not of this world of selfish, discordant, sensual men, for ye have been called to the Higher Life, where peace reigns evermore.

Ye are bound by indissoluble chains of love, and not by the bonds of the flesh, of avarice, of selfishness, and of passion, wherewith the people of the Outer World are bound.

Love knows no evil, and only seeks to bless all.

I would not condemn those who have not the light of the spirit, and walk by the uncertain light of the flesh alone. They are Otmar, ones who have not awakened to the newer light of the spirit.

They are neither to be condemned nor pitied. They are walking where ye walked ages ago. The divine spark will yet be kindled upon the altar of their souls, and then the path of the spirit will be made plain and clear to them.

Hold condemnation for no man. Be not so conceited as to think ye are higher or wiser than others. The veil has simply become thin between your eyes and the Infinite Omn.

As brothers, commune together and enjoy the serenity of a pure and noble life.

Walk among men, imparting of your peace and love to those in need, and your influence for good shall be felt afar in the world. Then shall thy soul become as sweet and fragrant as the air of morning, and Peace and Love the wings that bear thee onward amid circling spheres of light.

CHAPTER III.

PURPLE and gold are the mountains of Sebas-thā-ontu; above hang wavy billows of golden fleece; for he that giveth life to all terrestrial things, mighty Thā, sleeps in the Chamber of the West.

The valleys are filled with purple mists and gloom, for the arrows of Thā no longer speed on their course.

The night winds laden with the heavy perfume of a thousand plants soothe the restless breast of man, and seal down his eyelids with a kiss.

Sleep, the shadow of death, is abroad in the land, and all is quiet, save the shrill note of the night bird and the voices of innumerable insects.

Behold the grandeur of the heavens! The crown that Omn wears sparkling with innumerable gems.

The soul is filled with awe and reverence at the majesty of the scene.

All that the natural eye beholds pales into insignificance before the illimitable depths and numberless globes of amethyst, purple and gold that burst upon the bewildered vision of the spirit.

Who made these chariots of fire that circle forever the throne of the Infinite One?

Ever on and on! from chaos to nebulæ,—from nebulæ to suns, from suns to worlds!

Who the mighty Sculptor that shaped the endless variety of forms?

Who the mighty Artist with brush dipped in molten colors made the heavens shine with new lights unknown before?

What mighty Musician gave to each star and sun its keynote, and made the heavens vocal with a new song voicing the majesty and glory of the One, Everlasting Omn?

The Heavens give answer: Our Creator is Spirit.

Archangels are the servants of Omn. They, the framers and builders of universes. They, the sculptors, artists, musicians, incomparable.

In their hands chaos assumes form. The lightnings are their playthings. All the mighty and subtle forces obey the mandates of their wills.

They make the pathways for circling spheres of fire. They determine when worlds shall be born out of these spheres, and shape and fashion them into things of exquisite beauty.

Their work completed, angels of light are placed over them and become the masters of their destiny.

Innumerable spirits do the biddings of these angels. And thus from angels to spirits, and from spirits to man terrestrial, throbs and beats forever the Life that is that of the Eternal One.

One Life in all and through all! One purpose, that of the Divine Will, pulsates in every atom, making through all a most perfect undertone of harmony.

Purple and gold are the mountains of Sebas-thā-ontu, as the shades of evening settle over the earth. Peace, sweet peace, spreads her wings over all, and the questioning spirit of man rests ere it takes again its upward flight.

CHAPTER IV.

THUS spake Zertoulem: Worlds age; suns grow cold and cease to give forth light; both return to chaos whence they had birth.

Their substance never ceases to exist; but the form it had been compelled to take is no more in the external world.

There are only two conditions of life, although the manifestations may be infinite—the External, or outer, and the Internal.

The first is the realm of shadows, reflections of spirit as it passes across the great stage of Infinite Action.

The second is the realm of the real—the spirit that vitalizes all things.

Awful beyond description the spectacle of dead world or sun rushing madly onward into the wide opening arms of chaos.

Sublime beyond description the birth of a sun out from the dark clouds of chaos and night.

With quickened vision the seer sees beyond world or sun the all-powerful arms of spirit that hurled to destruction or quickened into life.

Over the formless he beholds a sphere of pure amethyst light. Innumerable rays flash from this sphere, grasping the dead atoms and impregnating them with life. The atoms thus vitalized rush together and a sun is born into the universe.

Beyond the sphere of light the seer beholds the form of the Archangel. But his eyes are still veiled, for it is not given to mortal to behold all the glory of those who stand nearest to the Infinite Omn.

All power belongs to spirit. Here lies all that is permanent. Elsewhere all is fleeting and delusive.

He who sets his heart on earthly things is unwise, for these in time must return to the formless.

Rather think of those imperishable things of the spirit, for these abide with thee evermore.

Too great love of earthly things deadens all the nobler instincts of the spirit.

Much earthly possessions anchor the spirit to the earth. These impedimenta must be removed before spirit can spread its wings for flight into the Higher Heavens.

Infinite possibilities slumber in every human soul. These are wrought out through many incarnations.

Ye may have already trod the dust of many worlds.

But he of little faith says: If this be true why do I not recall previous embodiments?

In answer, Zertoulem would say: Many do dimly see as in a glass the faint shadows of past experiences. But life holds within itself the results of all experiences.

It is wise to assert what the spirit perceives; and he who is ready to receive will accept.

The prophet speaks for all men—but all men are not yet ready to receive his words.

Be patient, if the world receives not thy message; if it be of the spirit, thou canst afford to bide thy time, for sooner or later the world will listen for thy voice.

CHAPTER V.

SPIRIT is not born, therefore dies not. It is individualized not as a whole, but as a part of the Infinite One.

Each soul possesses an atom of the Supreme Consciousness. This atom possesses the power to attract other atoms to itself.

Inasmuch as the outward body is a matter of growth and development, so also the inner body, or that which becomes the envelope of the spirit after its transition from mundane life, is made up out of emanations from the thought life.

Spirit is a segregation of divine atoms. These atoms never lose their relationship to the Infinite One.

The Infinite One is more than father and mother, brother and sister, wife and husband, children and friends, for it is all of these and more.

The air taken into the lungs gives new life and tone to the physical body. Inflate, then, the lungs of thy soul and draw from the Infinite Reservoir more atoms throbbing and pulsating with the life that is divine.

Death holds his carnival only in the external world. He cannot cross the threshold of spirit.

Things created alone come within his domain. The realm of the uncreate lies beyond his reach.

Spirit triumphs over the grave and charnel-house. It is the only victor that fears no conqueror.

It counts not time either by years or cycles, for it knows only the ever-present Now, which is Eternity.

As in the realm of the external those things that approach the nearest to the imponderables are the mightiest of all, so in the internal world spirit is the power that controls all.

Think of the external life, then, as only one incident along the endless journey of spirit.

And know this much of the future—it holds divine possibilities in store for all.

Think not that there are favored ones of the Infinite, unless all are favored ones.

Even the meanest life holds its measure of sacredness, and even here the struggle of the good for supremacy is apparent.

The divinest life cannot hold more than its measure will contain of that which maketh for righteousness.

Omn is not a jealous God; neither does He love the few and hate the many. Over all are stretched His protecting arms; all bask in the sunshine of His love.

Oh, Omn, our souls reflect the light and glory of Thy presence!

Our souls are ever filled with devotion to Thee, the one true God, whose love is the source of our growth and strength.

We would worship Thee through sacrifices placed on humanity's altar.

Deeds, and not words alone, are the gifts we would bring unto Thee.

Oh, may the world learn the lesson of sacrifice, and love season humanity's every act!

CHAPTER VI.

NEONTU asked Zertoulem, What is Religion? The Master plucked a wayside flower, and turning to Neontu, said: Perceivest thou this flower I hold in my hand? How beautiful in form and color! And how exquisite its fragrance! Man with all his art and skill could not make one of these. It has taken Nature millions of years to prepare the condi-tions necessary for its development. Might we not almost call it the soul of the world?

Few there are who truly understand the nature of religion. Far too often the world takes the outward form for the real essence of religion.

Religion is more than belief and its attendant ceremonies.

It is the flower of the soul, whose expanding petals are Charity, and whose fragrance is Love.

Like as millions of years were required to make the flower I hold in my hand, and Nature broke and threw away many moulds before this flower came, so the soul has discarded many forms of religion that served their day and purpose, before the Higher Religion was found.

The petals of true Charity seasoned with Mercy and Justice shall be for the healing of the nations.

The all-abiding fragrance of Love shall cement all races and peoples into one great brotherhood.

Without religion the soul wanders darkling in eternal night.

With religion it rises to celestial heights and basks in the light of the Infinite One.

As the body requires food, shelter and raiment for its sustenance, likewise the soul needeth spiritual food.

In the silence findeth the soul the food it needeth the most, for there only is perfect communion with Omn.

All that harasses and perplexes the soul is made clear, for the soul then perceives that the undeviating path leadeth to victory at last.

Through religion is revealed the at-one-ment with the Infinite One.

In its widespread and sheltering arms it holds the tired heads of all humanity.

Over the troubled waters of restless ones its voice cries out, " Be still," and the waters are troubled no more, and the souls rest in peace and harmony.

Here the tired and weary ones of earth find rest; and those who have been disposed to do evil are led to perceive the true light that in time will guide every soul to peace and righteousness.

Not creed, not outward ceremony, not pious cant, is that religion that leadeth to a more devout and holy life; but it is the pure white flower of Charity, whose fragrance is Love.

Hasten the day, oh, Omn, when man shall turn from the outward symbols, and the mammon worship of the hour, to the things of the spirit that giveth life, and to the acceptance of Charity and Love as the basis upon which religion needs must rest.

CHAPTER VII.

NO longer is anything new unto me. Surprise never overtakes me. For back of all outward forms I perceive spirit, that produces all things.

I have stood with universes without number; have assisted at many births celestial and have watched with calm, unwavering spirit the breaking up of worlds and suns into the formless chaos out of which they had their birth.

Life is that which gives motion and unrest; being withdrawn all things fall into Not-Being, the formless, primeval chaos.

Spirit and life are one—or, rather, life is the manifestation of spirit.

We are told that there are mineral, vegetable and animal life; but these are all one, differing only in the intensity of vibration.

The more rapid the vibration the nearer we approach to the pure white light in which Omn forever drapes himself.

As in music vibrations determine the note, so in man vibrations determine the degree of spiritual growth and culture.

Ask not the man of low vibrations to the feast where falls the manna of Heaven, for he is not yet ready to assimilate such food.

Spread for him the rich viands of the earth, for he is of the earth, earthy, and has hardly risen above the vibrations of the mineral world.

Invite unto the spiritual feast those who knock at the door.

Despise not those who are yet in the valley, and see not for fogs and mists the light and beauty of the mountain tops.

Remember, once thou mayst have stood where they are standing, and with feeble vision failed to pierce the thick clouds that were around thee.

Unmindful of what others may think move onward, ever obeying the voice within, and nothing shall prevail against thee.

What are the riches of the world compared with those of the spirit? Like as the flower perishes in a day, so these shall not remain after this day has faded into the All that Is.

Poverty is more of a blessing than a curse. It is the fire of purification that sublimates and strengthens the soul, and prepares it for a fitting habitation of the spirit.

At the gate that opens upon celestial glories, he who was poorest in worldly goods may find himself richer than he who was the possessor of much lands and worldly goods.

Yet despise not riches, and turn not away from worldly possessions.

Not the possession of these things condemns the man, but the uses he makes of them.

If he clings to these things that his appetites and passions may be gratified, then they become stumbling blocks along his path.

But if he uses them for his own and others' welfare, they will become stepping stones to the higher.

Each man's spirit must determine the uses to be made of all things. Obey the Voice that speaketh when all other voices are silent, and all will be well with thee.

CHAPTER VIII.

I speak the universal language of the spirit, and in time all men will hear me and understand. The language of the spirit translates itself into all dialects.

The stars speak the same language to all men, yet are they ever understood, for the truths they voice are heard of the spirit.

Likewise the prophet uses the universal language of spirit.

If he spake in one dialect his message would be lost to many men. But if he speaks in that which is universal his message is never lost.

He strikes the chords of sympathy and love that must vibrate in time in every human soul.

He does not stop to argue, but from the heights he has attained announces what he perceives to be true.

He is above all controversy, and will not discuss that which he knows to be true.

Out of the many discussions and controversies of men come the Babel-like confusion apparent in the so-called sciences and religions of the world.

The prophet calls to his own, and his own know his voice.

What if he dwells on mountain heights? He is not afar from the hearts and souls of men. For the spirit knows neither space nor time.

He draws unto himself those who are led of the spirit to approach him.

His voice unto them is like sweetest music and his words are the wingéd arrows of love.

His thought finds lodgment in their souls and produces in due time the harvest of perfected lives.

The strongholds of ignorance and superstition are overthrown from within and not from without.

The world throws aside its old garments no longer of service to humanity.

Customs outgrown, rites once held to be sacred disappear simply because the vitalizing spirit is withdrawn.

Foolish is the man who has no more profitable labor than to batter down the old.

Leave it alone and soon it will fall, for spirit is slowly but surely withdrawing from it.

Speak boldly thy message to the world! Not as one angered with thy fellow-men, but as one whose heart is fired with love and goodwill.

Then shall thy words live in the world, and thy message become a living power that leads to good.

One might as well find fault with the snail because he travels not with the fleetness of the horse as with the theologians whose eyes see no glory save that of the past.

In time the snail will acquire the agility and fleetness of the horse, but it may be millions of years hence. Nature does not censure the snail, but awaits with patience its slow but inevitable progress.

Then, oh, man, be possessed of the patience of Nature. Wait, and thou shalt perceive that the theologian has felt the thrill of eternal progress.

If thou art a prophet of the soul thou shalt perceive what is to be, and the equanimity of thy soul shall not be disturbed by the slow progress of the world.

CHAPTER IX.

Rise, oh, my soul, to still loftier heights—

Unfettered be all thy wings!

Let earth's empurpled mountains fade upon my vision.

Rise, oh, my soul, to still loftier heights—

Unfettered be all thy wings!

Let the great sun sink and fade from out the heavens.

Rise, oh, my soul, to still loftier heights—

Unfettered be all thy wings!

Fade from my vision, oh, ye mighty worlds and suns, flaming with amber, and gold and purple light.

Rise, oh, my soul, to still loftier heights—

Unfettered be all thy wings!

Past the great abysses of the formless and the void where suns are born and worlds and suns sink in their graves.

Rise, oh, my soul, to still loftier heights—

Unfettered be all thy wings!

Through spaces limitless and heavens immeasurable I fain would wing my way.

Rise, oh, my soul, to still loftier heights—

Unfettered be all thy wings!

Through circling spheres of light where spirits and angels dwell I still would cleave my way.

Rise, oh, my soul, to still loftier heights—

Unfettered be all thy wings!

Past globes of dazzling brightness where earth's Messiahs live still would I wend my way.

Rise, oh, my soul, to still loftier heights—

Unfettered be all thy wings!

On, on, with maddening rush through trackless azure fields, thick sown with sparkling gems, on wings of love, oh, soul, pursue thy way.

Rise, oh, my soul, to still loftier heights—

Unfettered be all thy wings!

Swift, oh, soul, be thy onward flight beyond those white-lighted spheres where archangels dwell.

Rise, oh, my soul, to still loftier heights—

Unfettered be all thy wings!

Behold where dwell the sons of God in Infinite light and splendor.

Rise, oh, my soul, to still loftier heights—

Unfettered be all thy wings!

With bowed and reverent head approach the centre where dwells the Infinite Omn, whose splendor, beauty and glory no artist soul can depict.

Yet rise, oh, my soul, to loftier heights—

Unfettered be all thy wings!

Within thyself unfold all that thine enraptured spirit has beheld. Put from thee all that is unclean and impure!

Awake, oh, my soul, to loftier ideals!

Aroused be all thy latent powers!

Let thy destiny as revealed spur thee on to greater efforts, to nobler sacrifices!

Be clean, oh, soul; be pure, oh, soul!

Around thee shines the halo of immortal light!

Rise, then, oh, my soul, to loftier heights—

Unfettered be all thy wings!

CHAPTER X.

I proclaim the gospel of myself. Be ye not copies of me—but instead be ye first originals.

The light, although it may still be beautiful, is weakened by reflection.

Let the light that is within thee shine out through all the windows of thy soul.

Repeat not the thoughts of others, unless thy soul gives sanction to their verity.

Speak out what is within thee struggling for utterance. Not only speak out, but live out the thought within.

Say not thou art too poor for this, that, or the other. Thou art rich indeed if thou livest near to thine ideals.

And no man in all the world is so rich as he who lives out the life of the soul.

Be not content with the living of other people's thoughts. Let thine own life have an individuality all its own.

Every flower in the field lives its own life, reflects its own thoughts, externalizes the ideal of the spirit.

In the external life be like a crystal, reflecting the pure white light of spirit within.

The Schools declare: Think as we think, and we will place upon thee the seal of our approval.

Rather live without the approval of the Schools if to gain this prize thy reason and conscience are stultified.

Let nothing stand between thee and the light of thy soul.

Within the orbit of thy spirit revolve worlds, suns, stars, universes.

Spaces and times illimitable are thine own.

Then be ye masters of self.

Let not the soul be troubled by the discussions of the sects. Thou art superior to all sects, and the voice within will determine for thee what is right and best.

Once having found the way, walk with unfaltering footsteps therein.

Fear no evils, for what men call evils are but shadows of ignorance and superstition that fall across thy pathway that needs must fade into nothingness before the blazing light of spirit.

Men fail only when they attempt in their lives to copy others.

If thou art a musician, sink not thine individuality in the composition of the master, but instead give it thine own interpretation.

If thou art an artist, copy not the work of the master unless thou canst make it glow with the fervor of thine own soul.

If a sculptor, make the marble speak the highest ideals of the soul.

Be no mere copyist in whatever field of life thou occupiest.

Let the fervent passion of the soul be manifest even in the most trivial things of thy daily life.

Seek not to be like Zertoulem and to think his thoughts after him, unless these thoughts strike responsive chords in thy soul.

Then shall they awaken the dormant consciousness within that will reveal to thee thy true individuality.

CHAPTER XI.

UPHEAVALS toward perfection are met everywhere in the universe.

Yet matter has its metes and bounds; these are determined by indwelling spirit.

As the child fashions out of wet clay various forms and gives to them names that suit its fancy, so do the Archangels determine the forms world-stuff shall assume.

At the approach of these mighty geniuses the formless assume shape and the depths of space become vocal with the everlasting song of progress.

Trace the history of one globe and the march of progress is revealed.

All forms emerge from darkness into the light.

Night hangs her sable curtains before the enchanted chamber of transformation.

Darkness ever hides the formless, and light ever reveals the radiant forms of beauty.

For vast æons of time was the world preparing for the advent of man.

Myriad forms of life paved the way for his coming.

Every form of life prophesied the coming of the higher.

When man came, weak and lowly though he was, yet within his soul lay dormant infinite possibilities, and these declared his home from afar.

While through evolution may have come the outward man, yet the spirit was not born through the gates of many deaths, but came from the heights or depths of the universe, leaving behind the shining pathway of its glory.

Its mission to subdue and conquer a new world, to pass through struggles and experiences, that in time it may hold within itself the results of all experiences.

By devious pathways the spirit marches onward—its life here but one of its many expressions, and, although much of the life is seemingly unimportant and trivial, the whole is essential when viewed from celestial heights.

Ask not now the reason of certain experiences in life, but wait patiently until the revelation comes from the spirit within.

Grieve not over the past, and sigh not for lost opportunities. No opportunity that was really thine has ever been lost.

Let the Now be the better on account of the past. Rise, oh, soul, out of all thy shadows!

He who spends his time grieving and lamenting over the past lets the golden opportunities of the Now slip by unnoticed.

Arise, then: be not controlled and swayed by phantoms that stretch their hands from out the past. Be superior to all experiences, making all to serve the divine purposes of the spirit.

If ye stay in shadows it is because ye will to do so. The sunlight is as much yours as any one's. Then arise, oh, royal soul, and claim it as thine own.

That which is really thine no one can take away from thee. Thou mayst be deprived of chattels and lands, for these never were really thine own.

But the fruitage of the spirit, the results of many experiences, thine inheritance from the ages, is thine forever, and none can deprive thee of it.

CHAPTER XII.

HE who entertains the truly religious life and takes pleasure only in things spiritual has already become immortal.

That which is gross and material is not forbidden him, but instead he rises above it and it becomes repulsive to him.

From the eminence he has gained he can never fall, because he has gained it by his own efforts.

He will require less and less food for the support of his physical body because he draws more and more of his sustenance from the *akasa*, or ether.

Through sublimation the outward is becoming more and more rarefied, and the spirit, asserting itself more and more, scintillates through and around the outward in an aura suffused with a blending of amethyst and topaz light.

Through efforts of the will he arises to those heights where disease and suffering are known no more.

The body is swayed by mental states as the trees of the forest are rocked by hurricanes.

Let thy mental states be peaceful ones, free from anger, hate, selfishness and thoughts of disease, and health shall be thine.

Thy power is infinite; then, why be conquered by things which are inferior to thee?

Let them have no place in thy mind. Drive them out with higher and worthier thoughts.

Think health, live in the atmosphere of health, and thou shalt be strong and well.

Thought is the mighty sculptor that shapes and fashions thy body. By individual effort thou canst bring it completely under the control of the will.

Learn the secret of concentration, and all that the soul desires shall be thine.

Keep a fixed purpose in thy mind, and no matter how unattainable it may seem to the world, in time it shall be thine.

Nothing can withstand the power of spirit. The soul possesses the power of drawing unto itself everything it needs.

Sayest thou that the one thing needed lies afar in the depths of space, and thinkest thou the spirit cannot reach it and draw it unto itself?

Be not too certain of this, for the spirit knows neither time nor space. That which seemeth to thy finite vision afar, may be near unto the spirit.

Not only does the spirit recognize its own but it calls its own unto itself.

What ye would have, strive after, and in time it shall be thine.

But the wise man strives after that which is good and pure, and these things become the bright gems that stud the crowns of immortal spirits.

CHAPTER XIII.

LET not thy heart be troubled; thou believest in God, believe also in thyself.

Think not I speak of the outward, the transitory and fleeting, but of that which is as permanent as the Eternal One.

Thine own self is changeless, deathless, and in expression ever new.

The expression is not thyself, more than the coat is the real man.

Yet the coat is impregnated with the individuality of the man.

Likewise the expression hints of that which caused it to be.

Beautiful, indeed, are the clouds at the rising and setting of mighty Thā.

Yet are they but a feeble expression of the ineffable glory that caused them to be.

Beautiful, indeed, may be these temples which are one of the expressions of the inner self, but it is not for mortal pen to portray the beauty and glory that creates.

Infinite are the possibilities of thyself. Dost think the works of art beautiful? Genius has produced them all.

What, then, is genius but the awakening of thyself?

Sleep, and the world sleeps with thee! Awake, and the world echoes and reëchoes the voiceless song of the soul.

Admire the sculptured form, the painted canvas, the evoked harmonies of the musician, and think that these may all come out of thyself, even as they have come out of other selves.

No genius has yet sounded the depths, nor scaled the heights of the soul's possibilities. Say not when ye look at the products of art:

I would that I had created thee! Rather, become thou the creator, not of what thou seest in the external world, but of that which until thou camest this way had not been given outward expression.

Thyself hast been stultified by the teaching of the ages.

The cry has gone up from valley and mountain top: Conform! Conform! Paint as painted the masters. And even music, the most wayward child of human genius, hath been confined within the narrow walls of man-made rules. Only they who have scorned all rules have reached the heights and ravished the souls of men with celestial harmonies.

Listen well; be sure thou catchest the low-breathed intonations of thyself—and then voice them to the world.

What matters it if thy voice is not heard amid the Babel sounds of earth? If thou art true to thyself, thy voice shall still speak on in the world, and they for whom it hath a message shall hear and receive.

Thyself shalt call to thee thine own.

Be not impatient with others who fail to grasp the import of thy message, but still be true to thyself and speak right on, and thy thought shall yet help to shape the destiny of the world.

CHAPTER XIV.

HOW unwise to say: How substantial and real is matter?

For matter is only a state of that which is substantial and real, an expression of energy.

Truly may it be said, matter is the appearance and not the reality.

Matter is ever changing, assuming many forms.

The substantial and real is unchanging and without form.

The undying energy of the universes is without form or shadow of variableness.

He alone establishes all things. He alone of all things is permanent, eternal, infinite.

From Him all things proceed and unto Him all shall yet return.

I do not say that it is unwise to study the external that ye may know something of the house in which spirit dwells. Yet, would I ask, Is it not far better for man to know the real than the appearance?

The child busies itself with blocks of wood, building houses and castles as his fancy may direct. So the man of science far too often busies himself with things of no greater value, those that belong to the outer rim of things.

Would it not be wiser if he would seek the fountain-head, the source whence all proceed?

Yet, I would not be dictatorial, for each man must determine for himself the path he shall pursue.

Some will ever choose the longer way that leadeth at last to the truth; while others perceive the open way that leadeth straight as an arrow flieth to the coveted goal.

It is not necessary for them who perceive the truth to linger in the valley because the many are not ready for the journey that leadeth to the heights where Peace dwells.

Once having fully recognized the power of the spirit, all power is thine to overcome and utilize the seeming obstacles of the world.

What were yesterday thine infirmities may become to-day the source of thy strength.

An error once conquered never shows its head to thyself again.

Ye are all children of the light, and darkness is your abiding place only through ignorance.

Be ye not obedient slaves to circumstances and conditions, but rise in the majesty of thy spirit, superior to all that hinders thy upward flight.

Live in the Higher Thought thyself thinkest—bask not only in the sunshine of spirit, but, in a measure, be that sunshine unto others, who are yet in the thick clouds of ignorance, and thou shalt rise higher and higher as the spirit ever wills.

Then, to thyself there shall be no other thought, save that of peace and love; and from out thine atmosphere shall melt all thought of evil and disease, as the fogs and mists melt from the earthly atmosphere at the coming of the morning sun.

Then, in spirit find the mighty solvent that dissipates all clouds that have obscured the inner vision.

CHAPTER XV.

INTO the Silence, oh, soul, would I walk with thee. Into that chamber whose walls are adorned with the unexpressed ideals of the soul.

Here are thoughts that never yet were given outward expression.

Here are poems excelling in beauty and grandeur those of earth's greatest masters.

Songs sweeter and diviner than the incomparable Wagner ever voiced to an astounded world.

Here are thoughts more creative than those of the great philosophies and religions.

For now we have crossed the threshold of the unexpressed.

In the Silence characters are formed and developed.

In the Silence geniuses are born.

Out of the infinite depths of Silence proceeds all that is.

When I walk with thee, oh, soul, into the Silence, awe and reverence abide with me.

For that which is formless, uncreated, ready for the Master fills me with awe.

Stand I thus in the Silence in the presence of Depths abysmal and fronting immeasurable Heights.

The waters from the great Depths surround me. Plunge, oh, soul, beneath the mighty surging waves, and come up out of them purified.

Cleave with thy wings, oh, soul, the ethers that encircle the Heights, and be glorified by the light that glows and plays forever above their summits.

Into the Silence and commune with self; find there thy mission in the world.

There let the message come to thee that thou shalt give unto those who have become seekers after the light.

Into the Silence, oh, soul, and there find the glowing pathway of the spirit.

Humble though thy work may be, lowly thy mission in the world, in the Silence thou shalt learn its meaning, and thy soul shall be content to labor and to wait.

In the Silence great truths shall come to thee and thy soul be blessed with the rich increase of celestial knowledge.

In the Silence all perplexities shall vanish, all troubles shall cease, all sorrow be assuaged.

In the Silence the clouds shall lift, and the light that is ineffable encompass thy soul.

In the Silence thy soul shall find its own, and commune with the loved in the voiceless language of the soul.

From the Silence, oh, soul, thou shalt return, seeking no longer far and wide thy mission in the world, for the message of thyself in glowing and burning eloquence speaks in thine every act.

CHAPTER XVI.

ONE asked the Master: What shall be the nature of our homes in the world of the Lomkatos?

Just then Zertoulem came near to a shallow pool of water, and he stooped and picked up a pebble from his path and cast it into the water, and it sank out of sight in the slimy ooze at its bottom.

Then he turned toward the one who asked the question and replied as follows:

Behold, how the stone cast from my hand into the pool makes for itself a place in the slime and ooze under the water. Ye might at first think that my hand gave it the bed in which it should lie, but this is so only in seeming. My hand imparted the force that hurled the stone into the water, but the stone formed and shaped its own bed. The stone was spherical in shape and the bed in which it lies adapted itself to the shape of the stone. If the stone had been rough or angular in shape, its abiding place would have been the same.

Now, it was neither my hand, nor the force behind the hand that shaped the bed in which the stone lies. But, as ye can readily perceive, it was the stone that shaped its own bed.

Now, in speaking of the Lomkatos, the superficial observer might say, Inasmuch as Omn takes the spirit out of the terrestrial life, he must of necessity make the home in which it shall abide. How unwise this conclusion! Omn simply takes hence the spirit, but the power that hurls the spirit out of the physical body does not determine either the house or world in which it shall dwell.

If I ride in the chariot, neither the chariot nor the horse determines the direction I shall go. My spirit determines this and guides the horse and chariot accordingly.

So is it with the Lomkatos. The houses in which they dwell are moulded out of the deeds and thoughts that gave prominence to the lives they lived here.

Truly, we ought to be familiar with the nature of that world into which we shall be called to enter, for it has been builded up out of our desires and motives.

Special acts have greater effects upon the bodies of the Lomkatos than upon the worlds in which they shall live.

Desires and motives are the stuffs out of which their worlds are builded.

A world undesired and toward which no strong motive draws the soul would prove most unprofitable to the Lomkatos.

As the object of that life is not for sense gratification, but for intellectual and spiritual growth, it needs must follow close upon the confines of this terrestrial life and yet prove more fully adapted to all the soul's needs.

Easy are the gradations that lead upward in the land to which they have gone.

Well may it be called the land where all the desires of the soul are fulfilled, the land where the motives that underlaid the acts of the past become the stepping stones of the spirit.

Each one of the Lomkatos becomes the architect of his own home.

CHAPTER XVII.

THINK ye that life is not worth the living because it is a ceaseless struggle after the unattained?

Because so many of thy hopes and aspirations fall to the ground seemingly fruitless?

If thou thinkest thus thy view is narrow and limited.

How know ye that thy hopes and aspirations are fruitless?

May not their branches extend so far above thy head that their fruits are beyond the circle of thy vision?

Trouble not the limpid waters of thy soul with fear and doubt.

Cultivate that faith that leads to belief in the divine possibilities of the soul. And when I say the soul, I mean thy soul, every soul that is. For these possibilities are not for the few, but the all.

Life never can be a failure even in the poorest expressed soul of earth.

Even in the reeking haunts of vice and crime life is fulfilling its sacred and holy mission.

All life is sacred, holy, divine, but much of life is as yet poorly expressed.

As, in the world of music, not all are geniuses who touch chords that vibrate afar, so in the great world of the ordinary expression of life, the movement is slow and sluggish—yet, even in the meanest, it is an upward movement.

Sorrow, as well as joy, hath its mission in the world, for like the refiner's fire it purifies of all dross.

Thy desires are not attained! Thy hopes fall fruitless to the ground!

Stop, my child! As much of life lies before thee as is behind.

Why spend thy time in worthless grieving over the seeming failures of life, when eternity and all her years are thine?

That for which thou grievest to-day, to-morrow, laughingly, thou wilt throw aside.

Thy hopes dead! Thy desires unattained! Never was hope more alive than when clouds of sorrow come sweeping in upon thee. Never were thy desires nearer thy grasp.

Through the pearly gate of sorrow the soul rises on wings of triumph.

Hope is the bright star whose light gives the silver lining to every cloud.

Struggle on, brave soul; be not overcome with discontent. Look up, for lo! the morning dawns upon thee that dispels all shadows that have dimmed thy vision.

Be not led astray by the cunning sophistries of the world, the pessimism of the night that only points to chaos and to death. But follow the light within that points to the ultimate victory of knowledge over ignorance, and reveals good emanating out of all the evils of earth.

Over all tired and weary hearts Peace shall yet fold her wings and Love shall lull to quiet slumbers, out of which the soul shall awaken into that serene and perfect life that fully reveals the true worth of striving and living.

CHAPTER XVIII.

HOW beautiful is Life!

Radiant with the attributes divine!

How beautiful in its morning time,

When the jewels of innocence and purity sparkle upon its brow!

How sweet the prattle of childhood, like the murmur of the laughing brook!

Tireless its outgoing, and tireless its incoming;

For the springs of life are near whence it is perpetually fed.

Rosy-tinted are thy visions, for thy young heart yet knows no guile.

Thy breath is as fragrant as the air of morning, for thou hast brought with thee the odors of innumerable celestial flowers.

Indeed, thou art an angel from some distant star. Earth is not thy home, only thy resting place for a morning and an evening of thy life.

How beautiful is Life!

Radiant with attributes divine!

How beautiful in those days that give expression to perfected manhood and womanhood.

Reason, like a star, sitteth upon thy brow, and Love guideth the every act of thy hands.

Thy limbs have the strength of giants, and thy body the beauty and loveliness of a god.

Thy intellect scintillates afar its rays of light, for knowledge is the crown that graces thy brow.

Thy feet are upon the earth, but thy head towers aloft where heavenly breezes are ever playing.

Indeed, thou art a god given human expression, for in thee only that which is noblest and best finds a lasting abiding place.

How beautiful is Life!

Radiant with attributes divine!

When the snows and frosts of many winters have settled upon thy head, and the outer shell worn so thin that the pure white light of the spirit permeates and radiates through it all, how much more beautiful than e'er before thou art become, oh, Life!

Thy beauties now are all of the spirit. Thy life nearer the ideal thou hast ever been chasing throughout the long journey that lies behind thee.

A ripened sheaf; yea, thou art indeed a garner house of divinest wisdom.

The glory of a new day like a halo rests upon thy brow, and thine eyes are wistfully gazing towards the sunset for some sign or token that thy faithful spirit nears its home.

The music thy soul hears is not that of earth, but of voices long lost to thine earthly hearing, calling thee to thy home in the heavens, the well-merited reward of a life that has been well and nobly spent.

How beautiful is Life!

Radiant with attributes divine!

With tear-dimmed eyes we watch thee as amid the glories of the upper ethers thou meltest from our sight.

CHAPTER XIX.

THE Illuminated One is he whose spiritual faculties have all been quickened. This the one whose illumination is perfect. Of course there are many degrees of illumination.

One faculty may be quickened into newer and higher life while all the others remain in their natural or in a dormant condition.

But when I say Illuminated One, I mean one whose faculties have been exalted or quickened.

He, truly, is an Avatar, for all knowledge is placed at his disposal.

Memory opens to him the door of all experiences in past embodiments.

Oft-times he uses knowledge that has been brought from afar.

Think not that all the knowledge revealed through illuminated ones was acquired either in one embodiment, or while attached to one world.

Spirit calls no world home, but has been a traveller from remotest time along an infinite journey.

Yet, caprice and fancy play no part in these wanderings.

Law controls all things, and order reigns throughout all universes.

The life that is is willed to be by Higher Powers.

What if some say, This is the only life, the first and last incarnation?

Do not stop to dispute with them. Thou canst not make them see as thou seest.

Wait, and they will grow to thy thought.

But keep not thy thought to thyself. Utter it in world language and it shall vibrate on and through the world until all prejudice shall be overcome, and souls shall become responsive to its harmonious notes.

Study thine own soul, ponder well its lessons, before thou art ready to accept the lessons that others may offer.

If thou art illuminated, thou wilt assimilate the food thy soul needs.

Give raiment, material food and shelter to the physical body, but give the soul unmeasured love and knowledge.

Open all the storehouses of Nature and wrench from her her time-honored secrets, ransack the universe if thou wilt in search of new truths, but if thou wilt only be patient and wait, these shall all come to thee.

For the soul knows its own and draws all things it wishes unto itself.

Be ye content with fewer things in the external world, and seek to draw unto thee the higher ideals of the spirit.

But despise not the means that leadeth to the coveted end.

Perform the duties of every-day life uncomplainingly, for these may be made the stepping stones to true spiritual growth.

CHAPTER XX.

I call no one great, unless I call all great.

Each fills his place in the great plan of Omn.

Each has come at his own time.

Some have travelled farther than others, have seen more, have heard more, have lived more than others.

And some who have seen much and heard much may not yet have been aroused so that they can comprehend the meaning of all that has been.

Not all that is within thee has yet been lived. For thou encirclest all things.

I condemn not the thief, the murderer, the adulterer, no more than I condemn the wild beast for its ferocity.

Thou shalt outgrow all things, poor troubled soul.

Are these things committed against thee, my brother? I grieve with thee, but I pity thee not. Rise above all annoyances; it is possible for thee to ascend where these things shall trouble thee no more.

I have come up through the ages, uncounted and untold. On many of the stars thou wilt find the imprint of my feet. Rest upon me ages and ages.

Still on! presses my indomitable and restless spirit.

Long have been my sleeps, yet longer by far have been my awakenings.

The memory of all, dim and illusive, save at the quickening of the spirit, is never present with me.

From the star-depths stretch the great all-powerful arms that have upheld me!

For my coming great indeed have been the preparations.

From star-dust to blazing sun all have labored for me.

Tenderly all have cared for me,—the erratic comet has smiled upon me, and great stars have given me their protecting love.

Room has always been made for me throughout all my journeyings.

Rocked in the cradle of the universe the stars have sung my infant soul to sleep.

Yet was that soul a child only in its expression, for countless cycles even then were its own.

On, ever on, has been its swift flight. And, as thou hast journeyed, angels and archangels have called unto thee from out the depths.

I am the unmeasured, bent on an endless journey.

Try not to follow me, for do thy best to keep my track, I shall ever elude thee.

Blaze out, oh, brother soul, among the stars and nebulæ thine own path.

I shall lead thee, but it shall be unto thyself.

I shall point the way, but it shall ever be unto thine own path.

See, the mountain heights, purple-misted and indistinct in the distance, they stand ready and waiting for thy feet to sink deep within their virgin soil.

Make delays if thou wilt, yet sooner or later thou shalt reach their summits, and thy soul exalted shall know the meaning of the thirst unquenched and the hunger unappeased.

CHAPTER XXI.

SING, oh, my soul, thy sweetest song!

Strife is but for a day, while love endures forever!

Over the miasma fields and swamps filled with dank and poisonous growths,

Let its clear sweet tones echo far and wide!

Over the valleys richly laden with flowers, fruit and grain;

Over the world's great cities, where discord and lust and strife are ever breeding;

Over the wretched haunts where the sunbeams never lick up the dews of night, where children live and work midst awful curses, discords, and fruits of riotous passion;

Send forth, oh, soul, thy noblest song!

And let love's sweet sunbeams disperse all clouds of gloom.

Into prison cells, into hospitals, into retreats, where'er dwarfed and stunted ones may dwell;

Into peasants' huts, into kingly palaces, into factories, where swarm earth's toiling millions;

Into the busy marts of men, where merchants bicker and strive for that which far oftener lays a curse than a blessing upon him who receives;

Into the great colleges and universities, where men oftener give their time and talents to the acquiring of that knowledge that leads more to strife and disquietude than to that peace and serenity which is the goal toward which all wisdom leads;

Into the churches, where the preaching and the living far too often fail to accord with one another;

Into the great battlefields, hells of discordant notes, agonizing cries, and shrieks of despair;

Yea, into all places man dwells, where either peace is not, or love may not yet abide;

Send forth, oh, soul, thy noblest song!

For where thy voice is heard, no discord is!

Not over the hills and mountains of the earth;

Not from star to star, where angels and archangels dwell;

Not up to the centre of things terrestrial and spiritual, where the ineffable light ever is;

But on through abysmal depths where darkness reigns;

Through hells mundane and supra-mundane, where souls are struggling upward; Where the light is just beginning to penetrate, and souls lethargic, shaking themselves free from chains and fetters, awake to the first faint glimmer of that which is to be their glorious destiny.

Then sing aloud, oh, soul!

Let thy voice be heard afar!

Send forth thy sweetest, noblest lay! Wake all the hills, and shake all the depths of earth.

Yea, tremble, oh, ye hills, at the sound of my voice!

For thy doom is sealed; hate and anger cannot withstand the all-conquering power of love that endureth forever!

CHAPTER XXII.

NEONTU said unto Zertoulem: Behold how the people suffer! Go into the homes of the people, likewise into the great hospitals and asylums, and the sights thou shalt see and the sounds thou shalt hear will make even one like thee think the world is anything but beautiful. My heart is sad within me and my soul is sick unto death at what it has seen and heard. Pray, tell me, is there any way to overcome all this suffering?

When he ceased speaking, Zertoulem said unto him: Oh, Neontu, has all my teaching been in vain? Have I not already told thee that pain and disease are to be conquered only through efforts of the will, and that back of the will lies the illimitable ocean of spirit, the source of all power?

Dost thou think that one may find a panacea for all human ills in the bottles and jars of the apothecary? That some of these things are palliative I most fully believe. But I would not look to them for the cure of disease any more than I would look to war for the cure of the lust of the nations. Health is the natural condition of the physical body when spirit fully asserts itself through all its members. When there are obstructions along the pathway of spirit they must be removed, else will pain declare the presence of disease. Spirit holds the atoms of matter together; when it is withdrawn, disintegration commences and the atoms fly apart. The struggle of these atoms to obtain their liberty is what causes the sensation of pain. As matter approaches the formless it becomes grotesque and repulsive in appearance.

When man not only learns the way but also walks therein, pain and disease shall be known no more.

Oh, Neontu, if thou shouldst suffer great pain, it would not be necessary for thee to have faith in me in order that I might relieve thee. The two things necessary are these—that I have faith in myself, and also believe that at my command is the exhaustless power of the Infinite One.

Bear in mind, oh, Neontu, also this important fact, that if thou art the possessor of the pearl without price, faith in the divine possibilities of thine own soul, thou wilt never need other physician than thyself.

Thou canst call unto thee from across the depths and over the heights All that Is.

If this power was not thine, thou couldst not be a son of the Infinite One.

If thou art that son, thy power can be no less.

When the world accepts these thoughts and lives them, the way to overcome pain, suffering and disease shall be made clear. Then the sons and daughters of earth shall walk forth clad in new garments of dazzling whiteness, for Truth and Love, Peace and Purity shall claim them as their own.

Until that day pain and suffering shall not be completely overcome.

Hold, oh, Neontu, the Higher Thought, and from thy soul, and also from all noble souls, let its vibrations stream forth until the last groan of agony shall cease and hells on earth be no more.

CHAPTER XXIII.

WHAT sayest thou, Neontu, that thou hast fallen away from the Higher Thought? Nay, nay, say not so, because it is not, cannot be true.

Rather say that the Higher Thought never was thine own

For once Mine, always thine!

If thou perceiveth the truth and graspeth it with the firm hand of ownership, thou canst not fall away from it.

Never didst thou fully perceive the truth and grasp its full meaning, if thou thinkest that thou hast fallen away from it.

Yet it hath not entered into thee and become a part of thy very life, for if it had thou couldst not think that thou hadst fallen away.

Thou hast only reached its outer rim, and thy senses have become intoxicated with its fragrance.

When thou shalt perceive its inherent beauty and recognize its real worth thou canst no longer say that thou hast fallen from the Higher Thought.

Thought becomes higher and higher only as its vibrations are intensified by the spirit that creates it.

If its vibrations are sluggish it hugs the earth. If rapid it cleaves the ethers.

Thy soul selects that which affinitizes with itself, and cannot fall from that which is on its own level.

Thou dost not yet fully believe in thyself. Cultivate, then, oh, Neontu, a more thorough knowledge of thy soul.

Know of its possibilities limitless and its resources exhaustless.

Do not read the limitations of the physical into the atmosphere of the soul.

But read all that the soul is or yet may become into the physical.

As the moon is ever faithful to the sun, daily receiving and transmitting its light, so should the body ever be true to the soul, receiving and transmitting its light.

The soul is not fettered by metes and bounds—if thou dwellest in its world thy vision shall be limitless, and thy powers infinite.

Give not to these thoughts merely the assent of the intellect, for that availeth little.

But if thou canst receive them let them sweep through thee with all the power of conviction.

Then are they truly thine, and thou canst no more fall away from them than the earth can fall out of the solar system, of which it is an integral part.

It has been with thee, oh, Neontu, as with many others. Thou hast tried in vain to grasp the whole as a whole, before thou hast mastered its separate parts.

Step by step, degree by degree, must the neophyte move forward until adeptship is attained.

Through the gates of Meditation and Concentration thou shalt proceed, until at last Truth's golden crown shall grace thy brow.

CHAPTER XXIV.

THERE are so many opinions abroad in the world, asked Neontu, how can one know the right?

The Master replied in substance as follows: There are many rights, and it concerns thee only to know that which is right for thyself.

Be not troubled with the opinions of men. Thine own opinion is of more value to thee than that of any other.

That which is right for thee to-day may not be right on the morrow.

There can be for thee only one right, that on which the Now places the seal of its approval.

In thy childhood it was both right and good for thee to have playthings, but grown to manhood thou hast ceased to take interest in such things and it is right no longer for thee to have them.

Yet there are many men who have not advanced beyond their childhood days and are ever content with things of the past.

In science many men are content to while away their time in the study of the external universe, and never cross the border where Titanic forces are ever playing.

In religion the masses care only for that which comes up out of the grave of the past.

It is right for the man of science to deal with the externals until his soul is quickened into new life by the touch of all-pervading spirit.

It is also right for the devotee at the shrine of religion to bow at the altars that contain nothing but ashes of the past until his soul shall glow and flame with the light of the newer faith that proclaims Universal Brotherhood.

That which shows thee the more excellent way is best for thee and is always right.

Even in the midst of the confusion of the world thou canst always determine what is best, for that which thy soul approves is right for thee.

Each flower, herb and tree takes out of the soil only those elements needed for its growth and complete unfoldment. Each is too busy about its own work to stop to discuss the other elements it leaves behind.

Why not learn a lesson from the vegetable kingdom? Out of the great mass of facts and theories offered in the philosophies and religions of the world, the soul should select those that appeal to the Inner Consciousness, neither accepting nor rejecting the remainder, but leaving them inviolate for those to whom they appeal.

I denounce no science, no philosophy, no religion.

One might as well kick with bared foot the wayside nettles; they would not be harmed, but thy foot would be stung.

I declare nothing is false for others. I only affirm what is right for myself.

Then, oh, Neontu, test all sciences, all philosophies, all religions, by the light of thine own soul, and if they are for thee, are right for thee to hold, they shall be drawn unto thee, and no amount of disputation can dispossess thee of them.

CHAPTER XXV.

THE world declares, oh, Death, that thou art cruel and relentless. That thy mission is to shatter and destroy all that it holds of the beautiful.

That thou lovest to wound the mother-heart, and to rock and sway the proud father-heart with grief that will not be assuaged.

That thou bringest to one common level those whom the world respects and loves and those whom the world styles its outcasts.

That all hearts are vulnerable to thine arrows, and each form matter assumes must bow before thy stern decree.

Speaketh the world wisely?

Thy vision must be obscured and all thy spiritual faculties blunted, or thou wouldst not speak as thou hast spoken.

Thou art neither cruel nor relentless, oh, Death, for thy mission is one of love and not of anger.

Thou art, indeed, the most beautiful of all the messengers of Omn!

Thou art not as poets and artists have pictured thee: old, haggard and terrible.

Thy cheeks have stolen the roseate tints of the morn; thou art as graceful in all thy movements as the fawns, and thy features reflect nothing more terrible than peace and love!

Thy mission is not that of destruction more than it is that of re-creation.

The golden bowl that held the prize of life is broken only that the spirit might find elsewhere a more glorious setting.

The temple that had grown too small to hold longer its proud inmate has fallen—but there are other temples more spacious and beautiful awaiting the advent of the soul.

Oh, Death, thou hast given a broader liberty, a more glorious freedom to the soul.

Thy door swings inward, noiselessly opening upon enchanted chambers radiant with unwonted light and glory such as earth hath never known.

Thou kissest down the eyelids in sleep, oh, Death, and imprinteth upon the lips the seal of immortality.

Beautiful, indeed, at thy gentle touch bath been the awakening into newer experiences.

Not, as some have said, into a new life, for it is the same old life that has unfalteringly kept its march through the ages, but thou hast simply brought it a little nearer to its ideals.

Behold the great company with which the soul now stands! For the call of the spirit has been answered, and its own have come at its bidding.

New fields lie open before thee, loftier heights than e'er thy feet have scaled stretch on and on before thee, oh, soul.

Death hath not robbed thee of thy treasures, oh, soul. All the good that thou hast done, all the noble thoughts thou hast expressed, live and are with thee still.

Instead of Death thou shouldst be called Life, for thou holdest within thy hands the keys that unlock the doors of space and time.

CHAPTER XXVI.

I am tired and sick of the cry, I can't do this and I can't do that. The world cares only for what thou canst do.

Show the world, then, that thou art capable of doing something.

No man ruled by "I can't" ever amounted to anything.

It is possible for the man who says "I can" to conquer and rule the world.

Receive then, oh, soul, thine own message! Be true to its light and the shadow of "Can't" will never cross thy pathway.

Art thou merely a creature of circumstances, ruled in all thy thoughts and actions by the stars?

Shame on thee, if such be thy thought! Arise in the dignity of the god thou art intended to be, and rule in the universe that is thine own.

Instead of thou being subject to the stars, they should obey the mandates of thy will.

The sturdy oak-tree, sound at its core, is rocked and swayed by the hurricane that sweeps over it, but when the storm has passed, undaunted it lifts once more its branches toward the heavens.

Thou mayst be rocked and swayed, oh, man, by influences both mundane and celestial, but learn to keep the equipoise of the soul.

Many times thou wilt be disturbed by others even in the life thou art living. Remember thou mayst disturb others.

Let these disturbances and these annoyances fall off from thee. Rise, and in the majesty of thy spirit show that thou art superior to these things.

Neither the pleasant nor the unpleasant things are the all-important ones in life. As results tower aloft above all experiences, so do motives become by far more important than acts.

Trials are good for thee when thou art not conquered by them. They lift the curtains to many a window and reveal in part the workings of the soul within.

Be patient; the universe was not made by thee, neither were the men and women in it.

Let them alone, to either live their own lives or become victims of unseen vampires.

It is enough for thee to look out for thine own life, for it is a most difficult thing to keep clear from all the snares that surround thee.

Rise out of the realm of *I can't* into that of I can, and then shall all the divine possibilities of the soul be revealed unto thee.

Only truth should sway and bend thee; only the wings of love and mercy uplift thee, and only justice dictate thy course.

Out of strife shall come peace, and out of the performance of the most unpleasant and unwelcome duties of life come rest to thy soul.

CHAPTER XXVII.

INASMUCH as the higher spiritual states are those of Wisdom and Love, so may the earthly states approach unto these.

If thou art self-centred thou canst draw near unto these gates of Light even when thou art in the midst of seeming discord.

It is not necessary that all men should behold the Light of the Love and Wisdom spheres that thou shouldst perceive it.

One may know with the mortal mind and not perceive with the spirit.

That which a man knows may never enter into his life of the spirit, but that which he perceives must sooner or later be incorporated into his very self.

Knowledge is no more than a bundle of dry facts and the understanding of a few laws and their application in the realm of use, unless the perception of the spirit gives to it life.

Perception of the spirit is an offspring of Love and Wisdom.

Love and Wisdom are expressions of the one great underlying energy of the universe, which is known as spirit.

Thus are we led to perceive in all things a divine unity reaching from stardust to man, and from man to the highest expression of the Infinite.

In mortal conditions all that is usually known as Love should be called selfishness. Here too often it is expressed in favors, a kind of coin placed at compound interest.

But there are times and instances when true love is manifested, for instance, as revealed in the display of heroism and sacrifice by the mother for her offspring, and, likewise, in every noble act and effort on the part of one for another.

Love's fires are not dead on earth, although covered far too often by the ashes of selfishness.

True love is an attribute of the soul that leaps upward like fire from the heart of the volcano, illuminating far and wide the night whose sky is overcast with clouds of hate and discord.

This is a reflection of the Light that forever plays about the heights where angels, Sons of God, Messiahs and Archangels have their abiding place.

And Wisdom is not merely the acquiring of knowledge, but also the understanding of its practical uses.

The Wisdom Soul is not only the one that knows, but also the one who perceives the value of truth.

How many there are of the earth children who have simply buried themselves in the dry details of technical science!

How many there are who have gathered, analyzed and classified flowers, insects and fossils, yet know not their uses in the Di- vine Economy of Things, and, with equal truth it might be declared, know not of that Divine life that throbs and pulsates through them all.

While mere earthly knowledge may be con- fined to the realm of physical data, Wisdom has its wings ever spread for flight into the realms of Cause and Use.

Thus clouds are dissipated, difficulties over- come, and the pure white Light of Spirit reveals the path that leadeth on forevermore!

CHAPTER XXVIII.

NEONTU asked the Master: Why is it that I am affected by all individuals that come into my presence, not only mentally but also physically? Some give me the sensations of peace and joy, while others almost completely destroy my equilibrium? It is not necessary for me to come into mental communion with people to be thus affected, neither is it necessary for me to come into physical contact with them.

The Master walked some little distance by the side of Neontu before replying to his interrogations. All this time he was noting the change that was rapidly stealing over the physical body of his companion. When they met that morning Neontu's body was terribly agitated, as if all the chords of his being were swept by a storm. But now all the nerve currents were calmed and brought under the control of the peace-loving Soul that dwelt within.

Then spake the Master: A moment ago, oh, Neontu, thou wast restless as an untamed steed, but now thou art calm as a philosopher. These conditions have been brought about by the mental states of others. Thou hast seen some delicate piece of mechanism affected not only by every change of temperature but also by every passing cloud. The most sensitive and delicate piece of mechanism when compared with the human body is crude and unresponsive. Not only one but many spirits may cause this sounding board to vibrate. Ever the dominant chord should be struck from within. But through ignorance and lack of spiritual growth it is often struck from without. Therefore the body is often swayed by other mental states than those of its own spirit.

Understand, oh, Neontu, that everything in the universe has its own aura. Rocks, trees, flowers, animals and human beings, each have the characteristic aura. We have now only to deal with auras of human beings. The color and nature of this aura is determined by the mental and moral states of the individual. In the gross and sensual it is dark and repulsive; around the purely intellectual it is blue; those reaching toward the spiritual, golden; and the truly spiritual, of dazzling whiteness. Generally speaking, no person is all gross and sensual, and no one in the physical body at all times purely intellectual or spiritual. Therefore in the aura of every person there must be a blending of different colors. The predominating color determines the bent of the individual. In disturbed mental states the aura is disturbed. In anger the aura becomes dark and through these clouds are fitful flashes of flame-colored light. At other times love sways the whole being and the aura takes on the roseate tints of the morning. These auras extend perceptibly about three feet in every direction from the individual. But the sphere of their influence no one yet has been able to measure. So, Neontu, when thou comest into the presence of individuals of pronounced mental states, thou art affected by their auras.

Protection can only come from within. Thou must be self-centred and self-poised; thy will upon its throne, and thine own aura well defined by deeds in keeping with the higher attributes of the spirit.

CHAPTER XXIX.

AS in the wild-wood there is a great variety of form, color and odor of the flowers we meet with, so is it with the auras of human beings.

Some of the flowers are regular and beautiful in form, others irregular, and some few apparently distorted.

So is it with auras of individuals; some are exquisitely beautiful in design, others very commonplace, and still others almost without form.

Some of the flowers in color rival the rainbow, others are modest and nearly neutral, while still others are murky and dark.

We have already seen that it is the same with the auras of human beings.

Among the flowers there are those that emit odors that are ravishing and almost entrancing, others are pungent, and still others are repulsive.

It is even so of human auras.

The so-called criminal, brutal and sensual class emit odors characteristic of the individuals, which are repulsive in their nature.

Many individuals of strong character, yet not specially inclined either to Intellectuality or Spirituality, emit a pungent odor possessing in no great degree either the power to attract or repel.

The intellectually inclined emit an odor very similar to that of the modest little flower known as mignonette.

And those highly developed spiritually emit odors that exert a magic spell upon all who come within the sphere of their influence.

These characteristic odors are not of the outer, physical body, but belong to the sphere of human auras.

There are undertones or musical notes to be discovered in connection with these auras.

Those who have not yet awakened to the knowledge of the better-self send forth discordant notes that ever fail to blend and to produce harmony.

There are those who live quiet, peaceful, unassuming and unpretentious lives, the waves of whose auras are ever vibrating with low, soft and sweet melody.

There are also those grand souls, ever struggling upward, ever breaking away from all restraints, ever promoting the higher interests of humanity, these are surrounded by auras vibrating with the grand, triumphal notes of victory.

With physical eyes you may not behold all these colors and forms; with physical ears you may not catch all these notes,—for in the universe there are forms and colors invisible to the physical eye of man, and notes either too low or too high to be heard by his external ears.

These truths can appeal, then, only to the spiritually awakened, for these have both heard and seen many things all unknown and unperceived by those who have not risen above the valley mists of materiality.

Then, oh, Neontu, let the real Neontu, not that which appears or seems to be the Neontu, assert itself, and thou shalt be led out of the world of shadows, into the world of light, where all things may be revealed unto the waiting spirit.

CHAPTER XXX.

YEA, Neontu, I did say, One Life throbs and pulsates through all from star-dust on through man up to the Infinite, a kind of vital spirit making out of the infinite variety of forms a divine unity.

Yet, I did not intend to imply that man was not more than star-dust. He is all the outer universe implies and infinitely more, for in external worlds there can be neither perception nor apperception. The star-dust of itself is not conscious of the existence of man, cannot reason with regard to things, neither can it grasp intuitively eternal verities, nor realize the power of Soul.

There is a power within thee, oh, man, possessed not by other things. While the Infinite Omn breathes in and through all things, yet His majesty unspeakable is only revealed in the spirit of man.

All else in nature has limitations. Consciousness, reason, intuition—these three reveal that which is absolutely limitless in its capacities and powers.

The ignorant alone place metes and bounds to the possibilities of spirit.

Thus far shalt thou go, is the command of unreason.

Thus far canst thou go, is the assertion of one whose interior consciousness has never been aloft on the wings of intuition.

If in thee a fragment of the Absolute and Real finds an abiding place, thou must of necessity be limitless in all thy powers and capacities, for the Absolute and Real cannot be composed of limited and circumscribed fragments.

The true poet, artist, musician are prophet souls, that never bide the limitations of religions and schools.

New paths of light are opened unto them and they walk forth where mortal feet have never pressed before. When they return they bring with them the rich vintage of the spirit.

The world, filled with self-conceit and blinded by ignorance, cries out: Our most sacred things are violated—our usages and customs ignored—these are but false prophets that needs must lead the unsophisticated astray.

Hold thy peace, oh, brother, thou who dwellest in the valley, thou art not yet aware that the sun is up; through the dense fogs of thine own pride and ignorance thou failest to perceive that the mountain tops are already bathed with the light of a new day.

Only a little longer canst thou stay where thou art. Through the thick clouds around thee hands are reaching toward thee that sooner or later will impart a quickening impulse to thy soul.

Light will yet break around thee, and the message of the spirit be made known unto thee.

Then clouds shall disappear—earthly taints of anger, selfishness and distrust be superseded by peace, love and confidence—and the Divinity within be revealed in its infinite glory.

CHAPTER XXXI.

'Tis well for every one to seek spiritual gifts, but it is far better first for every one to know his own spirit and something of its possibilities.

First let character, the sweet flower of the soul, be well developed.

It is to the man or woman what the perfume is to the flower, a revelation of the soul-life within.

The characterless man is always vacillating, never certain of anything.

The man of character is far more stable than the rock-ribs of the earth.

He is never swayed save by influences that lead either to his own or others' good.

His voice is like the deep, rich, melodious tones of the organ.

And through his whole life sweeps the rhythm of the universe.

To such an one is revealed the Divine attributes of the soul, possibilities beyond the comprehension of him who dwells in the valley land of vacillation and selfishness.

The gifts he seeks are above the plane of sense, and are not confined to those that take form and shape in the realms of materiality, but instead, pertain to the spheres of Wisdom and Love, therefore lead to the uplifting and spiritualizing of all humanity.

He does not deny physical phenomena as gifts of the spirit, for they may have been the rungs in the ladder up which he has been slowly and painfully climbing through the lapse of years.

But, as far as he is concerned, they have served their day and purpose. After a man has acquired a knowledge of geometry, calculus and the higher mathematics, he does not need to dwell longer in the realm of its first principles. He is far too wise either to deny their existence or to remain bound by the magic charm of their influence. Therefore he leaves the study of the self-evident truths upon which the science is founded for the neophyte. So ever must it be with psychic science. Those living in closest relationship with the sense-plane can only be reached through the cruder manifestations.

That ye may not be led astray by these into snares and pitfalls innumerable see that thy reason is alert, thy character well developed, and thy higher spiritual nature awakened.

Seek ye the higher gifts of the spirit, but seek through living nearer and nearer to the higher and better self.

If simply the doors are open unto the realm of sense ye need not expect to hear the entrancing music of the spheres.

Thou needst not stop to close the doors behind thee, for they close of their own accord when influences from the realms into which they open cease to reach and affect thee.

Be sure the doors are never closed before thee through thine own selfishness and lack of true spirituality.

They of the higher spheres will minister unto thee, if thou in word or deed art worthy of their ministrations.

CHAPTER XXXII.

LET no sound of martial strain be heard throughout thy world, oh, soul! March not forth with banners flying and trumpets echoing afar.

Let not, oh, soul, thy path be strewn with human wrecks and tortured forms.

Let not thy way be o'er earthly battlefields gory with human blood.

Let not thy onward course be paved with hopes and aspirations lost.

Let not splendor of outward expression dim the inner light and glory. Strike,

then, the grandest note of all, of peace and love to all mankind.

Over all the strife and discord of the world then let this thought prevail—

Peace, soft, sweet, like fleecy night-clouds.

Enfolding and enwrapping all in folds of perfect trust and love!

Light ineffable, glorious, all-potent, yet soft and silent as that of distant star, slowly, yet surely, lifting every soul out of the dark and dismal earthly hells.

Angels, not blaming earth's wayward ones, but with tender, loving arms encircling all, rescuing from maelstroms of anger and passion; supporting tottering footsteps along life's wearisome way, until, at last, the soul is quickened, and the master spirit asserts itself.

Not the assertion of self in the merely outward expression of things through martial power, brutal strength, and accumulation of worldly goods.

But that only real and true assertion of self that is forgetful of all outward expressions, resultants of power, strength, and worldly goods, save as they lead to the higher interests and greater benefits of the many.

Light, dispelling clouds of ignorance, removing obstacles, overcoming difficulties, making smooth the path where human feet needs must press;

Light, revealing unto enraptured vision new earths and new heavens, homes of contented and happy beings;

Light, making plain that which before perplexed and troubled;

Light, servant of spirits, angels and archangels, mighty and all-potent for human good when wisely directed;

Lead thou our spirits on,

From night unto day,

From discord and strife unto peace,

From selfishness unto that true love of self that can bide no ill unto others.

Lead thou our spirits on,

Away from charnel-houses of sin and death,

From battlefields and dismal prison cells,

From anger and hate's accursed fires,

Unto that love knowing no my nor mine save only that which leads to good of all.

Lead thou our spirits on,

Oh, light, messenger of Thā and Omn,

Through all the devious paths of life,

Thick-strewn with many a fret and care,

Until all clouds are gone, all strifes are gone,

And burn forever upon the altar of human hearts the fires of love and peace.

CHAPTER XXXIII.

THESE little jars and perturbations in everyday life simply emphasize the harmonies of the deeper spirit-life.

The All-Pervading Life that in time must overcome and master all things, in thy present life is only revealed by partial liftings of the veil.

No man knows its depth and full meaning.

For it is out of sight save when it flashes through the thick clouds which far too often enshroud the life of man.

Much of the disturbances in thy life are caused by outside influences.

That these may be avoided do not cut thyself off from others, for thy life of life must be associated with that of others.

Those that annoy and fret thee are always on a plane below thee. Intellectually they may be above thee, but always spiritually they are far beneath thee.

Cut not entirely loose from them, and yet be independent in thy way of living and thinking.

The light of thine own soul may arouse them to better things.

Nature's forces are silent until the work they seek to do is accomplished.

Say not thou art better or wiser than others, and, above all, pronounce not thy curse upon any one.

If any one hath done thee an injury, do thou no injury in return, for the first will never be righted by a second.

Poor mortal, thou art desirous of injuring another! Thou canst not afford to do it. The blow will fall upon thine own head with greater might than it does upon the one thou art seeking to injure.

Wouldst thou have friends in the world? Then be a friend to all men. Conquer thy meaner self, and let the spirit be more perfectly revealed each day of thy life.

Think not that thou shalt gain anything by striving to ride over others. Thy horses will balk and throw thee to the ground.

Be humble, not exalting thyself above others, and the true glory of thy higher spiritual nature will shine forth, blessing all humanity.

Then, if others seek to injure thee and put thee down, be not discouraged and disheartened.

But let thine own acts be seasoned with charity, justice and love, and in the end thou shalt arise in the majesty of thy spirit and be glorified in the presence of the highest.

CHAPTER XXXIV.

SPIRIT not only moulds and shapes the physical body which becomes its outward expression, but is also vibrating in its every atom.

If a part or portion of this outward expression of spirit is loaned another individualized spirit, the original creator of that part or portion never entirely disassociates itself from it.

In fact, the every atom called within the atmosphere of the indwelling spirit reflects in greater or less degree the attributes of that spirit.

Even when a member is loaned another, the personality whose vibrations are felt by the remotest atoms of the outward expression is never entirely submerged in the personality that usurps and controls the organ for the time being; therefore, in spite of every precaution, it flashes across the pathway of the thought being expressed.

But the spirit speaking cares little for this unless it may interfere with the expression of truth.

Then, is it not far wiser for men to be seekers after spiritual truths than for the evidences of special spirit control?

I that indite these papers speak far oftener for the many than for the one individuality known as Zertoulem.

What matters it whether the truth is found struggling in the mind of the medium, and is quickened into outward expression by the touch from without, or cometh entirely from an extraneous source?

The all-important thing is the clear perception of the truth.

Truth owns no special country as the land of its birth; neither the East nor the West can claim it as its own.

Prophet-souls in every land and every age have heard its voice.

Obedient to the message received, they have gone forth into the world as Heaven-sent messengers.

The truths they uttered in the long ages past have never been lost.

No word, no wisdom is lost past recovery.

Sigh not, then, over the esoteric wisdom of the past; if thou art ready for it, thou shalt receive it all.

It has been seemingly lost because the world was engrossed in material things, and had no time for those of the spirit.

Spirit needs no introduction to the ages past and gone. The ancient peoples are not stranger men and women to it, and the civilizations of old are not unknown to it.

It is for me and you to press the hands of these people, to walk with them shoulder to shoulder, to read with them the records of their struggles and triumphs, to reap the results of their civilizations, and to be exalted by the wisdom they possessed.

And this exaltation, not because the wisdom is ancient and belonged to a peculiar people, but because the wisdom contained within itself a spring of perpetual youth, and belongs neither to one age nor one people, but to eternity and to all men.

It is for thee to perceive as great truths as the world has ever perceived.

If thou wilt thou canst stand where the greatest have stood.

Thou must lift the clouds that hang over thee. Thou must plant thy feet firmly upon the earth beneath thee.

For it is not well to forget the needs of the outward, the external expression of spirit.

A god dwells within; the house should be beautiful and clean.

Through its every door should shine the ineffable light and glory of the exalted spirit, the inmate of the house not less beautiful.

CHAPTER XXXV.

HE who sends the healing thought is doubly blest, blest in giving that which others need, and blest in receiving that which he had not before.

Send forth no vacillating thought, freighted with the hope and trust for better conditions and higher things.

Instead, let thy thought be charged with the positive currents of love that know no defeat.

Hast thou not declared Omn to be omnipotent and omnipresent?

Believest thou this to be a truth? Then, inasmuch as thou art a part of the divine, all power centres in thee.

Thou art circumscribed and limited only by thy denials.

Ignorance builds up a wall that crumbles and falls at the approach of knowledge.

So all difficulties fade and disappear when one arises above the sphere of denial into that of affirmation.

When thou sittest in the silence to help or benefit another, concentrate thy mind upon the object to be accomplished. Be so desirous of doing good that no other thought shall possess thee.

Be not so foolish as to deny the existence of disease, poverty and sorrow, but affirm the possibility of rising above all that clogs or hampers the spirit.

Spirit, assert thyself!

Arise! shake off all that impedes thine upward progress.

Thou art creator of opportunities.

At thy bidding all the doors of knowledge are opened.

There are no secrets Nature holds that may not be revealed unto thee.

To the awakened soul there are no occult or hidden forces in nature. All are luminous with the light of spirit, and none are hidden save by the flimsy veil of ignorance.

Every breeze that sweeps over the land, every wave that beats against the shore, every ray of light that cometh from most distant star, has a message for thee, oh, man, if thou wilt only receive it.

Star-dust and earth-dust are one and the same, save only in the one the vibrations may be intenser than in the other.

On earth varied names are given to the so-called primal elements, but he whose spiritual vision is quickened perceives that there is but one substance in all universes.

Under all must be one,—that one we term spirit, the only substance.

Elements are the clothes that spirit wears. Hence all the varied forces are ever directed by spirit.

If the individual spirit is both self-conscious and self-centred, it calls other spirits to itself to aid in its every beneficent work.

A legion of spirits may do thy bidding if thy commands are wise and right.

A good thought speeding on its mission of love and beneficence calls to its aid the powers of many wise and good spirits.

Live above the atmosphere of ignoble thoughts and thy life will reflect only the noblest of impulses.

And these impulses shall be made to live in the lives of others.

They shall bring up out of despair, suffering and gloom those who never before have felt or known the sweet sunbursts of love.

In him from whom they proceed shall be wrought as great a transformation as in the ones they reach.

He who gives the most receives the most.

For angels are ever showering upon the head of the giver benedictions that are not of this world.

CHAPTER XXXVI.

REST, oh, my soul, not in the slumbers of the night,

Nor in the idleness that far too often accompanies the day,

But in the ceaseless doing of that which is right and good!

Out of turmoil and strife, thou shalt arise, oh, my soul;

And new courage and strength shall be given thee.

Fear not to trust that power within that with ceaseless urge presses thee ever onward!

Rest and peace can only come to thee, oh, soul, through ceaseless effort.

Sayst thou, the way is dark before thee, oh, soul, and thy feet have lost the way?

Nay, there are no lost trails, the path, though rough and strewn with obstacles, was thine own. The expression of thy life would have been incomplete without the discipline.

If thou wilt only learn the lesson these experiences hold thou wilt find rest even in the midst of the trials that beset thee.

Turmoil and strife about thee! Thy soul engulfed with waves of discord and inharmony. Complain, if thou must, until the soul perceives that divine wisdom underlies every experience of life.

I find no fault with thee because thou dost complain, for even this is required by the soul as it pursues its endless journey.

Rest may come in the midst of all this turmoil and strife, for peace shall abide with the soul when the meaning of all is made clear.

Art thou bereft of friends and loved ones? Doth sorrow rest heavily its hand upon thine aching head? And seeketh in vain thy tired spirit for rest?

Thou art not left alone! Thy friends and loved ones were never so near thee as now. All fetters broken, thy friends can draw nearer to thee than e'er before!

The sweet communion of spirit with spirit shall cool thy fevered and aching brow, and assuage thy sorrow. Thy heart bowed down shall beat again in ecstasy and love.

Rest shalt thou find, oh, soul, in the midst of that sorrow that produces the divinest of communion between spirit and spirit.

What more exalting and uplifting than the communion of spirit? Not with outward words of expression, but in the inward sense of things. No word is spoken. Thought leaps forth unexpressed save in the universal language of spirit.

What ecstasy more divine than when soul touches soul, and spirit reaches spirit through the limitless expanses of ether?

What a thrill of joy that is not born of the flesh pulsates through the interior consciousness!

Then thou art uplifted indeed! Thou hast scaled the spiritual Alps, and caught glimpses of things unspeakable and untranslatable into the language of the world.

Thou hast then, oh, soul, realized as ne'er before thy relationship with the One Eternal Omn!

Through all thy being waves of a new light have found their way, and rest, more perfect, more peaceful, than the soul has ever known before has come to thee.

Then, oh, soul, rest not in the slumbers of the night,

Nor in the idleness that far too often accompanies the day,

But in the all-pervading peace that cometh from the doing of that which is right and good,

Thou shalt fold thy wings in perfect rest.

CHAPTER XXXVII.

FROM spaces inconceivable, from depths beyond human comprehen-sion, from heights incalculable, voices call out to us, and hands reach down, through and up to us.

We are ministered unto by all that is.

Our way is not solitary and alone, even if our path is our own.

Innumerable the throng that attends us.

For us the beauty of the morn, and the glory of the expiring day.

For us the upheaval of earthquake and volcano, and the destruction that follows in the wake of the tornado.

For us the distant star emits its dim and misty light, and the comet flashes with fitful glare across the astounded heavens.

For us the herbs of the field, the proud and stately trees of the forest, and the humble lichen on the rock.

For us every form of life that peoples forest, stream, lake or ocean.

For us all movements, all rests, all strivings, all down-goings, and all uprisings, all emotions, all sympathies, all loves, all hates, all envies, all jealousies; in a word, all that is in part or in whole the expression of life, terrestrial or celestial.

These all wait upon us, minister unto us, and we through them gain the discipline needed for the higher spiritual attainment.

Then some might say, Why battle against the adverse? Why strive after the higher?

Brother, sister, know this and thou shalt question no more:

Vantage ground is only gained by battling and striving. The awakened soul is ever trying its wings.

The heights never come down to thee; thou must ascend unto them.

Omn speaks on and on evermore—yet His voice is only heard by those who listen for it.

Not in the external shall its sweetest and divinest song be heard, but only when man withdraws himself from all that belongs to the outward, and centres his whole life and thought upon that which is more than shadow, more than blazing sun, or world teeming with expressions of life, shall the soul be flooded with music whose notes are the vibrations of the light ineffable.

I would introduce thee to thy real self—the one very few in the world are acquainted with.

Thou hast lived so far away from thyself that thou hast become acquainted with its feeblest expressions.

Come ye nearer unto self—enter the holy of holies—the citadel whence consciousness proceeds. Behold the God upon the throne!

The real knowledge of self shall throw light upon others and make it possible for thee to sense the mission of each life.

Growth shall come from the possession of this knowledge, and through it shall come the understanding of the message that every expression of the All conveys to thee.

Through the darkness around thee shall flash the light that is not on land or sea, the light of spirit that ever lifteth to higher and better things.

And in the interior consciousness shall be made plain and clear the real meanings of the adverse experiences and the strivings that enter into thy life.

When thou shalt become submissive to indwelling spirit, all shall be fully understood.

For God knows all!

CHAPTER XXXVIII.

IF others near thee in the sense-world annoy thee, shut them out from thy real life. The ego may drive from itself all consciousness of that which it does not need.

The ego, the vital spark, that which is divine, dwells afar and apart from all that belongs to the external world.

It belongs to the depths, and not to the surface of things.

The *imago* and not the ego is incarnate. The ego builds for its creations houses, but these are not for itself to dwell in. One with the eternal, it is as houseless as the eternal.

It is well and right for thee to live much of the time apart from others, for in the interior consciousness thou shalt find all that is essential for thee.

Yet, leadings to this interior consciousness are necessary; books, men and things may be necessary to lead thee to thyself, but the time will come when these leadings will be needed no longer, for the dewdrop shall have touched the heart of the lotus and be merged in its interior consciousness.

He who walks through the world with his elbows in contact with other elbows never receives the leadings of the spirit.

Spirit needs neither props nor outside influences to make its mission known to thee. Its throne room is within, and only one can have audience at a time.

Thou must go alone if thou wouldst receive its blessings and commands.

Others cannot hear for thee; others cannot see for thee; others cannot receive for thee.

Spirit never calls two at a time. Its pathway does not admit of two walking abreast.

Through the same ethers and at the same times travel the varied forces of the universe, yet they never interfere with one another. Each is bent on its own mission.

In this world there is plenty of room for all, and there will be no jostling when all find their rightful places.

Yet, even as it is, the self-centred one is never disturbed.

Only those who are trying orbits that belong to others disturb and are disturbed.

Alone thou must be, and yet not alone, for the ethereal currents from interstellar spaces sweep around thee freighted with priceless cargoes.

Influences are about and with thee that know not earth as their home.

From all around thee Nature stretches out her hands encouragingly, and from above all power is showered upon thee.

Indeed, the favors of heaven are thine own, and thine associates kindred spirits from universes unnumbered.

Out of thine own sphere thou art hampered, cramped and besieged by forces, powers and influences that impede thy onward progress.

In thine own sphere thou art the ruler. Even the stars, nebulæ, universes lay their tribute at thy feet.

Indeed, the golden crown, sparkling with jewels, brighter and richer by far than the earth affords, sits gracefully upon the brow of the king who has become the ruler in the sphere of his own self-consciousness.

To him, all winds are alike; all experiences as they should be; all influences good; for all yield unto him a subtle essence that giveth strength and power.

None can bring evil unto him, for his feet walk the shining pathway of the spirit.

CHAPTER XXXIX.

MY soul is an hungered and it lifteth up its voice to the angels, yea, even unto the Infinite, pleading for food such as earth giveth not.

Every oracle and every book in the world faileth to give me the supply my soul needeth.

These all give freely of what they possess, yet my soul hungereth and thirsteth for the food and drink of the higher spheres.

The thirsty trees lick up the waters that fall from the heavens, and their hungry roots draw from Nature's breast sustenance, and they are satisfied.

Yet, oh, God, my spirit is never satisfied with what Nature giveth, no matter how bounteous the supply.

Even the granite rock crumbles to powder that it may feed the lichen that clings to its bosom.

And the great deeps hold a bounteous supply for all the myriad forms of life that swarm in their caverns.

I thirst, oh, God, for the great draughts of light that flood the upper heavens, and I hunger, oh, God, for the ripe fruitage of the ages.

Let me drink in the light that leaps from star to star, from universe to universe, until every chamber of my soul is flooded with unwonted light and glory.

Let the wisdom of the angels and archangels appease the hunger of my soul.

In the midst of darkness, surrounded by clouds of sable, I cry out for light! I stretch out my hands towards the heavens and I lift up mine eyes that they may behold the glory of Thy creations!

Worlds without number burst upon my vision; suns beyond human calculation flash and flame along the Eternal Ways.

Beneath all is dark, above all is light. Then, oh, my soul, be lifted up into realms celestial!

Let that calmness and peace steal over thee that the world on account of its passion and ignorance fails to receive.

As I cry out, voices from out the silence answer the voiceless cry of the spirit.

As I stretch out my hands the very heavens reach down toward me.

As I lift up mine eyes, lo, the heavens are ablaze with light for my spirit.

Truly may I cry out:

All, all that is, is for me!

The spaces are for me,

The light is for me, and

The Voiceless Silence mine own!

Blessed indeed am I, for all blessings are for me. If one helps my brother or sister, I am likewise helped.

Even in the remotest corner of the world a deed of kindness done unto the humblest of the children of men is done unto me.

Every good act, every good thought, no matter when or where uttered, blesses me.

I am not so narrow as to be blessed only by that which is done directly to me, but so broad that the universe alone is large enough for me, therefore, whatsoever of the good the universe holds touches me somewhere.

In me blend all races!

In me smoulder the loves and the aspirations of every age.

In me, the orator, the poet, the philosopher, the artist, the musician, the seer, the prophet—all either are now or have been expressed.

When I cry out for light, it is not so much for myself as for others, for the blessing comes not so much in the receiving as in the giving.

Like a crystal reflect all light that comes to thee, and then shall the light of thine own soul become more and more brilliant.

CHAPTER XL.

THE hills of earth rejoice, yea, the mountains shake their hoary heads with joy;

For a new religion is born unto the sons of men.

It is mightier by far than all other religions, for incorporated into it is the life of all.

The awakening of the real self has made this religion possible.

At present it only appeals unto the few whose souls are filled with divine fervor, but on the morrow, when the multitude awake from their long sleep, it shall appeal unto all.

Out of the peace and harmony of souls recognizing the real self and dwelling in the atmosphere of its consciousness must this religion spring forth.

These are the ones who recognize the beauty of truth as a whole and not simply in its fragmentary form.

The great ethnic religions contain only fragments of the truth. But these fragments are so beautiful that man has mistaken them for the whole truth.

Truth never dies, neither does it grow old; although changeless as the Eternal One, its aspects are ever changing.

The form it assumes is ever suited to the age in which it is presented.

Every religion that has outlived the age in which it was given to the world contains some fragment of truth of value to mankind.

If one searches long and patiently he may find this fragment of truth in every religion that still persists in the world.

In order that his researches may be rewarded he must be able to give a spiritual interpretation to the symbols and ceremonies associated with each and every form of religion.

Nothing lives in vain, and there must be a reason for all these religions living on in the world.

Truth being in all, the reason is found in the persistency of truth.

Now the world has waited long for a great cosmic religion that should absorb all the truth of the ages.

Not only has the world waited long for a religion that should absorb all truth, but also for a new setting of the truth that will adapt it to the intellectual, moral and spiritual demands of each and every age.

It has also waited for a religion that would appease the heart hunger of all ages, and also one that would contain within itself a fountain of perpetual inspiration.

Such a religion needs must be the centre of the thought and life of the world.

It must touch the humblest life as well as the most exalted.

Under its brooding wings even the meanest may find shelter and the way that leadeth at last unto peace.

To possess this religion in its fulness one must be able to find the oneness of self with the Infinite.

When he senses this royal kinship of the soul, he can cry out, I am not of this outward physical body, therefore birth, suffering, sensual attractions, death, are not mine, since I am as eternal and changeless as Omn!

This, the triumphant note of freedom that has rung down through the ages, heard and realized in its fulness by every awakened one of earth.

What Messiahs and sons of God have heard and realized all earth shall hear, and all her sons and daughters realize.

Not only do the hills of earth rejoice and the mountains shake their hoary heads, but all its plains and valleys vibrate with the new song of freedom at the birth of a religion that lifteth all, and not merely a few, into the realization of true manhood.

CHAPTER XLI.

THE Master continued: The new religion lightens every labor and will give rest to the weary ones of earth.

Does it not also reveal the fact that much of the labor of the world is both unnecessary and a hindrance to man's true spiritual growth?

Under the influence of this religion man should be led to want fewer things that belong to the external world, and only those things that conduce to the growth of his spiritual nature.

Under the new order of things works of art shall no longer be considered as either superfluities or luxuries simply to adorn the homes of wealth.

For then everything made by man will be a work of art. There can be no valid excuse for the existence of that which is ugly.

The time will come when it will be an unpardonable sin to create that which is not a work of art.

Man's labor becomes irksome only when he is forced to create that which is distasteful to him.

When everything that falls from his hands is a thing of beauty, his labor becomes one of love, and never rests heavily upon him.

Both the monotony and drudgery of everyday life oppress him.

Rest comes not in ceasing from labor, but from the doing of that which gives joy and satisfaction to the real self.

The new religion, taking a deep interest in the welfare of all mankind, seeks through art to elevate all.

In every one it reveals the God within, but, alas, too often looking out through stained-glass windows.

In time the stains shall all be removed from the windows, and then the real self in all its beauty shall stand revealed.

Until man's earthly condition is greatly improved we must look for spiritual illumination only in the few.

So long as man is looked upon merely as an animal, with no life save that of the physical, these conditions cannot be greatly altered.

All reform starts in the realm of the spiritual, and there, also, is found the greatest battleground of the opposition.

Not only the recognition of man's spiritual nature is a necessity of the hour, but also the recognition of the source of opposing forces and elements that antagonize everything that leads to the betterment of his condition.

The wise men, or seers, of Tlaskanata held that there were seven distinct and separate parts which united formed a human being. Commencing at the outward and proceeding towards the centre these parts arrange themselves after this plan:

1. The Physical Body.

2. The Vital Spark, or Life.

3. The Ethereal Form.

4. The Double Self, or, Will and Emotions.

5. The Mind—the home of Thoughts, Ideas, and Associations.

6. The Soul—that which as an Individuality is unaffected by death.

7. The breath of Omn.

In the self-centred one these separate parts are blended into the most perfect harmony.

The esoteric, or inner, meaning of religion stands revealed only unto those who realize this perfect harmony.

Those who are loaded down with the degrees of universities are generally too heavily weighted with the refuse ballast of the ages to rise to that altitude of soul-life where the secrets of Nature and of man alike are revealed.

CHAPTER XLII.

AGAIN the Master spake concerning religion as follows: Yea, I did say, oh, Neontu, that man had drifted away from God, and it was the purpose of religion to show him the trail that leadeth to the source of all wisdom and truth.

Man living in the sense-world is always in the midst of delusions. He lifts one veil from the face of Nature only to find another confronting him.

One mystery is made plain only to reveal a more inexplicable one.

Man will ever seek in vain in the realm of sensation for the cause of things.

Here he will find an infinite variety of forms—but the maker of these forms is ever out of sight.

That which eludes his grasp on the plane of sensation may be easily discovered on the astral and spiritual planes.

According to Tlaskan philosophy, the first four of the parts entering into the composition of man belong to the world of sensation, while the last three belong to the higher spiritual planes of thought and life.

By means of the first four parts he takes hold of the material side of the universe. These unite him with all mineral, vegetable and animal forms of life in all universes.

The transitory and delusive are ever weaving their web with finer and finer meshes around him.

Even the will is rocked and swayed by the emotions that oft-times have their birth in the realm of physical sensation.

It is a difficult task to classify the emotions, yet they may be readily divided into two great divisions. Those dominated by the passions may be known as physical emotions; those under the control of the higher attributes of the mind as love and wisdom emotions.

When the will is under the control of the physical emotions, or is hampered by these emotions, then man drifts away from all knowledge or conception of the Infinite.

When under the control of love and wisdom emotions he is led to perceive his relationship with the Divine.

It is the office of religion to cultivate these higher emotions, and thus lead man to the consciousness of his divine relationship.

But this consciousness can only come to the spiritually awakened.

Physical man can only know the manifestations of the absolute—but the soul may know the absolute, because in the soul the Breath of Omn, calm and steady in rhythmic vibrations, is ever ebbing and flowing like the tides of the sea.

Religion divested of all creedal associations will yet lead man to the realization of the higher self within, its relationship with the Infinite, and its possibility not only to conceive an ideal humanity, but also to bring about in the external world this long desired event.

Love is the only creative force of the universe with which religion deals. Love alone hath within itself the power to redeem, lift up and enlighten the world. Its fire once kindled upon the altar within burns on and on forever. From this fire religion borrows the Light that shall yet illuminate the whole world.

CHAPTER XLIII.

HOW strange that thou, Neontu, shouldst ask concerning the moral code of the new religion! For have I not again and again tried to make plain unto thee that ethical codes were of little value, because they can never usurp the place of that higher law known as that of conscience? While we may teach that right thought engenders right speech and right living, yet is it impossible to present a rule which followed by every man shall bring about such desired ends.

Each man must become a law unto himself. And when he recognizes that all strength and power comes from the Eternal then shall be revealed unto him the true path that leadeth to personal purity and righteousness.

Indeed, he has followed the true path a long way when he has learned that the consequence of every act must rest upon himself, and that no power will relieve him of this consequence.

The moral realm is as much the domain of cause and effect as is the physical realm.

Here no mediator stands ready to brush away the effects of long antecedent causes.

It may take many incarnations before these effects are all outgrown.

If ye sow the seeds of the distorted and spiny cactus ye cannot hope to see grow up out of the earth the graceful and well-proportioned tree. So must it ever be in thine everyday life. Love, wisdom and purity alone give strength of character and right expression to thine every act.

If man desires that which is good and true he will grow in no other direction.

If his desires are base, false and selfish his whole life will become either weak and vacillating or lashed into fury by the wild, boisterous waves of anger and passion.

Spiritual growth comes only when man is in most perfect harmony with all Nature—for then only can the better self be awakened.

If I were to give thee, oh, Neontu, one law to govern all the acts of thy life, it would be this:

Ever prove true to the light within!

What the soul affirms, as I have before stated, alone is right for thee.

The acts of thy life must conform to the dictations of the interior monitor.

The external should reflect the emotions, the hopes, and the aspirations of the higher nature.

When this is so thou shalt stand near to an immortality that is freed from the physical world.

To-day thou art suffering the consequences of acts in previous embodiments. In a great measure thou art the maker of thine own future.

All evil deeds must be expiated; all wrongs must be righted, for there is no forgiveness of sin.

Thou art both thine own judge and executioner.

Yet there is no escape for thee. The judge will be impartial and just, and the executioner will see that the sentence is duly carried out.

Then, is it not wiser for thee to cease thy mad, impetuous rush through life, and allow prudence and caution to exercise their benign influences over thine every act?

Through the gateway of thy new birth let not dark shadows stream forth from the tombs of the past.

Instead, may the golden beams radiating from noble acts and impulses make the smiles and laughter of the newborn prophetic of the incarnation upon which it is just entering.

CHAPTER XLIV.

NATURE unbosoms all her secrets to the votary at her shrine. But when the crude and materialistic approach, they find thick veils interposing between their eyes and spiritual realities.

To the physical scientist the spiritual side of Nature needs must remain a *terra incognita*, so long as he seeks to explain all phenomena by means of physical laws.

Simply because a man fails to understand the occult side of Nature, that is no reason why he should deride and ridicule those who have seen the light and know whence it cometh.

The wise man ridicules no one; accepts what appeals to his spiritual and intellectual nature, and leaves the rest for those who can make use of it.

To him Nature seems broken up into isolated points until the spiritual, that which unites them all into one perfect whole, stands revealed.

In order that one may have a correct apprehension of truth, it is necessary to know what has been as well as what now is, and also understand the *rationale* of the whole.

The problem of life will never be solved by investigations conducted solely on the physical plane.

Truly may it be said, only to the seer or mystic does the grain of sand unbosom all its secrets.

He who listens to the myriad voices of Nature patiently and long will be rewarded by hearing the low, soft, sweet undertone which is the voice of indwelling spirit.

Having heard the voice and interpreted its message, the man must become all that it imports before he can gain that freedom from animality that leads to true spirituality.

To him the gates of other worlds shall fly open, and the soul travel at will amid the splendors and glories of the Upper Worlds.

Not merely the thinking and the knowing that a thing is so, but the being that very thing gives this power to the soul.

Not all who knock at the temple and cry out, "Lo, I am here! Open unto me!" shall be received.

They only who have met and conquered the adverse experiences in life, and who have come up out of deep sorrows and the bitterest of tribulations, shall be admitted to the inmost mysteries.

These are they whose footprints are visible along the shores of time, whom the ages have crowned with the laurel wreath of the victor.

Indeed are they worthy of all truth, for they have been weighed in the balances of the ages, and have not been found wanting.

Thorns have pierced their brows, sharp stones their feet, envy and malice their souls.

Yet they have proven true to the light within; have ever obeyed the mandates of the spirit; have ministered to the poor and lowly; have bound up aching and bleeding hearts; and have caused the light of love to illuminate many a darkened pathway.

From the heights the angels cry out: Hail, all hail! Immortal and deathless soul! Thou hast completed the task, henceforth only the perfect form shall be thine own! Thou shalt blaze like a star at midnight, and thy light shall be like that of a beacon along the darksome way of so many human lives. Pursue thine ever onward journey from star to star, from universe to universe!

CHAPTER XLV.

IN vision of the spirit I beheld the man that is to be! He who wearily had climbed up through the ages until he had reached the summit of physical development.

Beneath him lay Error's mangled form and by its side that of Selfishness.

All the passions were under the control of the magic wand of Reason.

And even the emotions which to-day rock and sway the strongest of men bowed in humble allegiance to the indwelling consciousness.

No longer a creature of circumstances and a prey to the unseen vampires of the ethereal realms, for the inmate of this perfected form had become master of himself.

In the man of the yet-to-be, the spiritual nature in its unfoldment will always be in advance of the development of the physical.

All outward things are correspondences or results of things that are of the spirit—therefore the physical state is determined from within. All growth is from the centre toward the circumference, and man's physical body is not an exception to this law that obtains throughout all universes.

One of the most marvellous manifestations of spirit-power is presented in the physical development of this man.

Here the house will always indicate the nature and attributes of its inmate.

The mind encased in the physical body can hardly conceive of anything more beautiful than the perfected physical body, through which at times flashes the light of indwelling spirit.

Well may this house be termed a temple fit for the habitation of Omn!

Fresh from the Master's hands, perfect in the adjustment of all its parts, it throbs and pulsates with the all-pervading light that is eternal!

The fire that ever burns upon the altar of the soul has been kindled by the hand of Omn, and shall die out only when Omn ceases to glow and burn as the central fire of all universes.

Beneath his feet smoulder the fires of earthly lust, greed and selfishness, but over his head, like a coronet fit for an immortal god, glow forevermore the stars of Faith, Hope and Love.

Faith in all the true, beautiful and good time has gathered up as his most sacred treasure;

Hope, kindling the fires of Charity, inasmuch as it compels all to perceive that good is the final goal of all, and

Love, whose influence, the divinest of all, causeth man to work no evil, but to do good even to the humblest and meanest of all created things.

Blessed trinity, whose light shall become brighter and brighter in the world, until the love of my and mine shall be lost in that deeper love of the All, that shall foster in every human heart a sense of the brotherhood of all, that shall yet usher in the Golden Age foretold by seer and prophet of every race and age the world has seen or man has ever known.

The age when man shall own no master save that of his own spirit, bow at no altar save that over which the stars of Truth and Reason never set, and offer to the Unspeakable One only that worship which consists in the doing of that which is right and good.

Then shall appear what I beheld in the vision of the spirit as the man that is to be!

CHAPTER XLVI.

THEN spake Neontu: Oh, Master, I would seek the easier pathway. My feet are torn and bleeding, and my heart is sore from many a dagger thrust. Why labor for others to make their pathway easier while ours lies over the untrodden fields and up the steep and trackless ascents? The multitudes are but slaves that bow and kiss the hands that oppress whilst they either spurn or strike the hand outstretched to bless and assist them. Why not go on our way, as thou hast already taught, alone, and leave them to stumble along as best they may?

When Neontu ceased speaking, the Master turned toward him with a smile, and said: Oh, Neontu, how canst thou have ease of mind without freedom and self-government? And how canst thou obtain these unless thine every duty is performed? If the smallest duty is neglected ease cannot come to thee. The man who governs himself is the one who is willing to forego much of the so-called pleasure of the world provided that thereby his life may prove a blessing unto others. No man is self-centred and consequently self-governed unless he heeds every dictate of the soul. The soul speaks not merely for the one, but for the all.

No man can afford to have plenty while poverty is all about him, neither can a man afford to be negatively good and pure because he keeps himself away from all that is unclean and impure. The pure can touch and handle the impure and unclean and not be polluted thereby. Thou mayst infuse the best qualities of thy life into those who are impure and unclean, and thus be able to lead them step by step away from all that impedes the upward journey of the soul.

Can thy soul be at ease in any other walk of life than that which it prompts thee to take? Certainly, I did say, thou must blaze out thine own path, but whilst thou art doing that, nothing hinders thee from becoming a light unto others. Thou mayst lead them to a knowledge of self. Thou mayst lift the clouds that hang over them, and reveal the fire that burns forever on the altars of their souls. Thou canst not make the path for their feet to walk in, neither canst thou compel them to walk in any especial path. Thou mayst show them a more excellent way and thus become a means that leads to their advancement.

In the doing of good and also the leading of others to do good, thou wilt find ease thou canst not find, search as thou wilt, in any other way.

Thy feet torn and bleeding! If thou findest thy rightful path thy feet will not longer press upon thorns and jagged stones. If thou art only self-centred and self-governed, the poison arrows of malice and envy will no longer pierce thy heart. Thou art too firmly centred in thine own selfish desires to rise to those altitudes where malice and envy can harm thee no longer. Do the good and right not because thou expectest to be rewarded for thy services with the smiles and kindly words of the recipient, but because the doing of the good and right brings its own reward in the satisfaction it causes to permeate thy whole being. Stop not to think what others may say or do, for thou canst never find valid excuse for doing wrong in the thought that the multitudes love that which is evil.

Rise, oh, Neontu, to that sublime height of the soul where thou wilt no longer feel the waves of contention and strife rolling over thee, but by thee and around thee and through thee shall sweep the breath of Omn on its eternal way, bearing the message of peace and love to all souls who have conquered the lower nature and have attained the freedom that is that of the self-governed.

CHAPTER XLVII.

AGAIN my teachings have been misunderstood when thou sayest, oh, Neontu, that man should ever look inward. I have declared again and again that the source of all truth is within, but, at the same time, its streams are ever flowing outward toward the circumference. It is always well for thee to know the results that obtain in the physical domain. I have not found fault with the physical scientist because he studies the shell of the universe, but have tried to impress upon thee that it would be far wiser on his part if he would occasionally look within, and thus learn the source of all phenomena. Curb not the aspirations of thy nature that reach outwardly. Like ships sailing over unknown seas they may return laden with the richest of cargoes. Yet do I boldly declare unto thee that all the riches thou mayst be able to gather from the material realms will prove of little value unto thee unless thou art able to perceive in and through all the underlying spirit of all things. Here alone wilt thou be able to find permanency. The clothing thou wearest to protect thy body after a time is laid aside for new. And even the atoms that compose thy body are continually being discarded that their places may be given to others. The compelling power of all Nature that causes the ceaseless urge in every atom as well as in every flaming sun and star is spirit, the only Absolute Reality. Yet as spirit worketh in all, the humblest forms may teach thee important lessons. Ever have I sought to impress upon thee the sacredness of all things—that nothing is moving across the infinite stage of action aimless and purposeless. While I would not have thee ignore the organization, yet I would not have thee linger too long in the form-realm, for I would have thy spiritual sight opened, so that thou couldst behold the architect of each and every form. The form may be indeed beautiful, but far more beautiful is always the builder of that form. If ye delve simply amid the outward forms, mystery will ever enshroud all things. To thy vision the face of Nature will ever wear an impenetrable veil. But if thou wilt cultivate the interior senses, they that be of the spirit, it shall be thy privilege to lift the veil from the face of Nature, and in ecstacy almost divine, behold such beauty and glory as never before fell upon the vision of thy spirit.

It is true, oh, Neontu, that thou wouldst not have been placed in this outward world unless its lessons were of importance and value to thee.

Therefore it is well that thou shouldst become a close student of all the many things that surround thee, but at the same time thou shouldst not allow thyself to become so thoroughly entangled in the meshes of the web that Maya weaves around thee that thou canst not at any moment free thyself and soar on the pinions of the soul to those heights around which the ethers of the heavenly spheres are ever playing. Be not content to plod on thy way, grovelling ever in the midst of those conditions that hold thee in the sphere of materiality, but instead develop that higher spirituality at whose bidding shall open all the secret chambers of being.

CHAPTER XLVIII.

THE states after death are dependent upon the states before death. I have sought, whenever the opportunity offered, oh, Neontu, to impress upon thee the great law of consequences. In other words, that it is impossible for man to escape the consequence of his every act. Therefore, habits must necessarily cling to him after the body physical has been thrown aside. No miracle occurs to transform him in a moment's time from a demon to a saint. If his home has been in the realm of the carnal appetites and passions, death will not lift him out of that realm, for it can destroy only that through which these appetites and passions were gratified. Such spirits attach themselves as parasites to susceptible subjects, and through these usurped bodies seek to gratify their unhallowed desires. Inasmuch as there are malignant spirits encased in physical bodies, there are also malignant spirits denuded of physical habiliments, who disturb the equilibrium of everyday life, break down health and harass these physical bodies by sowing in them the seeds of disease. Much of the insanity of the world has been caused by unhappy suggestions and melancholy thoughts that emanate from these evil spirits that still hug the lower strata of physical life. Many times the holy sanctuary of life is not only invaded but also desecrated by these spirits. The rightful owner of the house for the time being is deposed and sometimes fairly driven away. The most powerful adversaries man is called upon to meet are they of the invisible realms. Because of their invisibility they are the more dangerous. Their attacks are all carefully arranged and planned without our knowledge. The powers and principalities thou art called upon to wrestle with are not of this world of physical sensations, but of the great realm of the unseen, out of which everything that is proceeds.

Not only are men directly controlled and influenced by these spirits, but the great social, political and religious worlds are invaded by them. Thus, oft-times are they enabled to wield a powerful influence over the affairs as well as the lives of men. Here may be found in part the cause of the perversions in the great religions of the world. The social and political conditions that obtain in the world are also in a great measure influenced by these denizens of the lower spheres.

Oft-times they invade the aura surrounding the sensitive and live on his very life. Through him they again live the old life, drink in once more its delights and revel in its associations.

This species of vampirism is far more prevalent in the world to-day than many are willing to believe. The great body of men and women who are prone to investigate along the line of psychical phenomena are ever ready to hear of all that which is good and beautiful, while they turn away in disgust from him who would show them the darker side of human existence. Man cannot afford to wander longer in the realm of half-truths. In order that he may be well armed and fully equipped for the battles of life he must know the whole truth. Therefore he must be led to realize the dangers that confront him. Knowledge is one of the greatest sources of our strength and power. Ignorance makes slaves of even the wisest of the earth. Ignorance draws dark curtains before the eyes of man, while spirit vampires creep upon him unawares. Knowledge lifts all curtains, dispels all fogs and clouds, revealing the enemy in his lair. When we know our enemy and the source of his strength, the battle is more than half won. Victory comes when we are led to realize our own strength and power.

CHAPTER XLIX.

WELL dost thou ask, oh, Neontu, How can we deal with these conditions? How free the unfortunate one of the parasites that have attached themselves to him? First, bear in mind this great truth: Occult Science never interferes with effects, but always seeks for the causes that lie behind them. The inner life, the realm of thoughts, emotions and desires, is of so great importance, since hence proceed all external conditions, that it demands from us more than a passing notice. Here centre all the forces that build up and replenish the physical body. Right thought, right emotion, right desire, must give a well-developed, properly nourished and well balanced physical body. Perversion of thought, emotion or desire gives the opposite. Out from the process of thinking spring the mental images with which we are surrounded. These images are our constant attendants. They take on the color and aspect of our thoughts. Our outward lives may be apparently pure; we may walk in the pathway that the world terms that of virtue, and yet know absolutely nothing of what real virtue and goodness consists. The mental images may assume the libidinous features of earth's most depraved, and with such images, the creations of our own thoughts, may we feed the smouldering fires of lust. Thus may the emotions and desires be turned from their legitimate channels. On the side of the lower self man is linked with all beneath him, while on the side of the Higher Self he claims kinship with angels and archangels. It is right here on the side of the lower self that man lays himself open to attacks from the evilly disposed. There must be not only bodily purity, but also mental purity, if we would be invulnerable to such attacks. On the side of the Higher Self man opens doors to divine possibilities, which are revealed in the realm of the interior good. If this one thought is fully grasped, thy questions, oh, Neontu, are completely answered. Lower conditions are never dealt with successfully on their own plane. One must deal either from above or within. To grapple with these conditions one must realize that he stands where neither the arrows of malice nor envy can reach him. His whole being must be charged with the knowledge of his superiority.

The unfortunate can be reached and res, cued from the meshes that have been woven around him, but it is necessary that his spirit shall be reached, awakened from its lethargy, and the mind encouraged to call into existence new images whose countenances shall reflect only love and goodness.

If thou art conscious of thy divine powers, and revolving in thine own orbit, possessed of right thoughts, right emotions and right desires, none can ever injure thee. Only those who have not found their rightful place in the universe and are not fully aware of their own powers are subject to the influence of those winds that blow across the marsh lands of the astral realms.

Be as firm and as unyielding in what thou knowest to be right as Truth itself; keep thy whole life near to the ideal thou hast set up before thee; let love lead thee ever with her gentle, yet firm, hand along the pathway that makes for true righteousness; then mayst thou walk forth as a god among men, fearing no evil, unharmed even in the midst of the vilest and most malicious of earth's children, for thou hast found the Perfect Way that leads to complete mastery of all things.

CHAPTER L.

OPEN, ye pearly gates that lead to eternal bliss! A soul imprisoned would seek the freedom of the Upper Spheres!

While yet enrobed in flesh, he fain would partake of the celestial viands and sip the nectar of the gods.

Thou art long in coming, oh, Death, and the soul, grown impatient at the delay, knocks at the gates of life eternal, demanding that they no longer keep it from its divine birthright.

Thou hast served me well, old body, moulded into most exquisite form from out the potter's clay. Through constant use and contact with the rough, wild elements of space and time thou hast grown more and more ethereal, each day reflecting more and more perfectly the workings of spirit within.

Soon thou shalt fall off from me as the leaves in autumn time fall from the trees of the forest. I would declare that thou hast been a most faithful servant, for most faithfully hast thou reflected all the fancies, caprices and imaginings of the arbitrary ruler who sits upon his throne within. I shall miss thee and drop a tear of sincere regret when the last vestige of thy form fades into the All of Nature.

Yet, whilst we two walk hand in hand together, I would peer out along that path the soul must take when we shall part company never to meet again.

Open, ye pearly gates! I knock! I knock! A soul imprisoned seeks to know the secrets of the Upper Spheres!

Silently, as the coming of the morn, the gates swing inward. A light sweeps by me in billowy waves that make all earthly light seem but shade and deepest shadow, revealing far, far off in the distance, mountains of amethyst, topaz, chrysolite, turquoise, flaming and flashing with light, leaping from peak to peak, on and on throughout the vast empyrean of heaven!

Filled with awe and reverence, my upturned eyes drink in the unspeakable glory of the celestial realms; trees with iridescent foliage; flowers that seem to express the very thought of the angels; seas of burnished gold and silver and soft greens and blues, and hanging dreamily over all fleecy clouds.

Here and there the eye beholds forms of divinest beauty, either speeding on errands of mercy and love or seeking mid the ever-changing forms about them the processes of their evolution.

Overcome with awe and reverence, the bewildered soul turns once more earthward.

For it is not yet prepared to dwell in the midst of such glory and magnificence. For it still must come the toil, the disappointments, the inharmonies of the sense-world, until all bonds are broken, all fetters loosened, and purified of all earthly dross it shall rise from sphere to sphere, ever nearer and nearer to the light ineffable that flashes on from century to century, from æon to æon, from time to eternity, the light that ever veils the countenance of the Eternal

Omn!!

TLASKAN WORDS

Akasa. The great ocean of ether sweeping in and through all things.

Lomkatos. Omn taken; those who have passed through the change called death.

Neontu. One of the disciples of Zertoulem most deeply loved by the Master.

Omn. The Eternal; God.

Otmar. Under clouds; not yet awakened to the light of the spirit.

Sebas-thā-ontu. Sebas, mountains; thā, the sun; ontu, setting. "The Mountains of the Setting Sun."

Thā. The sun.

Tlaskan. The sacred race that peopled a portion of Central America many thousands of years ago.

Tlaskanata. The Land of the Sacred Record; so called because the people were led to this land by a prophecy in their sacred writings.

www.ingramcontent.com/pod-product-compliance
Lightning Source LLC
Chambersburg PA
CBHW051549010526
44118CB00022B/2641